MW00849151

FISHERMEN SLAVES

HUMAN TRAFFICKING AND THE SEAFOOD WE EAT

Martha Mendoza, Robin McDowell, Margie Mason, Esther Htusan and The Associated Press

Mango Media
Miami
in collaboration with
The Associated Press

AP EDITIONS

AP Editions

Published by Mango Media, Inc.
www.mangomedia.us

This is a work of non-fiction adapted from articles and content by journalists of The Associated Press and published with permission.

FISHERMEN SLAVES *Human Trafficking and the Seafood We Eat*

ISBN: 978-1-63353-321-9

Publisher's Note

AP Editions brings together stories and photographs by the professional journalists of The Associated Press.

These stories are presented in their original form and are intended to provide a snapshot of history as the moments occurred.

We hope you enjoy these selections from the front lines of newsgathering.

"I'm very sad. I lose my eating appetite. I lose my sleep. They are building up an empire on slavery, on stealing, on fish(ing) out, on massive environmental destruction for a plate of seafood."

— Susi Pudjiastuti, Fisheries Minister, Indonesia.

Table of Contents

PREFACE

For hundreds of slaves, Benjina was the end of the world.

The remote Indonesian island village was cut off for several months a year due to stormy seas. There were no roads or telephone service and just a few hours of electricity a day.

The Burmese fishermen who docked here spent months at sea, pulling up monstrous nets and sorting seafood around the clock. But the relief they felt after touching land was quickly replaced by desperation. They were trapped, held captive by Thai boat captains working for large fishing companies. Some men were locked in a cage for simply asking to go home. Others who managed to run away were stuck on the island, living off the land for a decade or longer. And just off a beach, a jungle-covered graveyard was crammed with the corpses of friends and strangers buried under false names.

When AP reporters first arrived in Benjina in late November 2014, informing the men we were there to tell their stories, they couldn't believe it. A few wiped away tears as they spoke. Some chased after us on dusty paths, shoving pieces of paper into our hands with the names and addresses of their parents in Myanmar.

"Please," they begged. "Just tell them we're alive."

The long, sometimes dangerous, journey of telling the story of Southeast Asian men held captive on fishing trawlers began in late 2013.

Human trafficking in the global seafood industry had been written about anecdotally, but Associated Press reporters Robin McDowell and Margie Mason were determined to connect the dots in a way that would make the world finally take notice.

Their best bet, they decided, would be to link slave-caught fish to American dinner tables – and name names. At the start, sources told them it would be next to impossible. The industry was huge, and its practices murky. Fish was transferred between boats at sea. Documentation on land was often done improperly. And tainted and 'clean' seafood was mixed together at huge export markets.

Nearly a year into their investigation, they caught a major break. A source pointed them to eastern Indonesia, where they discovered a slave island.

AP reporter Robin McDowell

At great risk, McDowell, with the help of Burmese reporter Esther Htusan, filmed a man in a cage, and others pleading for help over the side of their giant trawler. The two also watched as fish was loaded onto a giant refrigerated cargo ship, and then tracked it by satellite to a Thai harbor. They were there with Mason to meet it in trucks, following the catch over several nights through the seedy, mafia-run streets. California-based reporter Martha Mendoza then joined forces to complete the four-woman team, eventually linking the seafood directly to U.S. supermarket chains and retailers, including Wal-Mart and Kroger.

The story captured worldwide attention. It led to governmental and corporate action. More importantly, it resulted in one of the biggest rescues of modern-day fishing slaves, with more than 2,000 men from four countries being identified and repatriated, some returning to homes they hadn't seen in 20 years.

This is their story.

The investigation begins: Mason and McDowell

Mason and McDowell spent nearly a year assessing the local seafood industry before locating Benjina. Their account:

Thailand is the world's third-largest seafood exporter, earning $7 billion annually. With a major shortage of workers willing to take the dangerous jobs, the business runs off of poor people from within the country, along with illegal migrants from neighboring Myanmar, Cambodia and Laos who are issued fake seafarer documents.

In the last decade, with depleting fish stocks at home, Thai boats started moving farther and farther from shore into foreign waters. After learning from a source that the number of Burmese fishermen stranded in Indonesia had been steadily rising over the past few years, we decided that was the place to look. We spent months scouring the Internet, poring through academic papers, networking and quietly reporting behind the scenes.

AP reporter Margie Mason

Our big break came when Jakarta-based Mason was told that stories of abuse were starting to filter in from the little-known island village of Benjina in the eastern part of the country. But because no outsiders had visited, it was impossible to know just how bad it was.

We got to work, finding two recent escapees and analyzing satellite imagery of a factory with dozens of fishing trawlers lined up like matchsticks in its harbor. McDowell headed to the scene.

On the ground: McDowell travels to Benjina

With preliminary research in hand, McDowell travelled 24 hours from her base in Yangon, Myanmar to the island village of Benjina with a team of reporters. Here's her account of that first trip:

When we arrived in Benjina, as a news organization, we had to register with police, saying we were doing a generic story on fishing. Four government minders were assigned to escort us wherever we went.

That made reporting difficult, but not impossible. While AP photographer Dita Alangkara and videographer Fadlan Syam toured an Indonesian-Thai fishing company with officials, I broke away. I thought the waterside brothels would be the best place to start looking for migrant fishermen, and I was right: The prostitutes said all of their customers were from the factory. Most were Burmese, spending the little money they were given every time they docked on booze and women.

Next, a local boatman named Eddy agreed to take me to coastal villages dotting the island so I could talk to fisherman who had escaped abusive conditions on ships or were abandoned by their captains. Again, most were Burmese. Though some were now married to local women and had children, all desperately wanted to go home. But with no form of identification, they were stuck. As illegal migrants, they knew if they went to authorities they could be arrested and thrown in jail. So they remained on the island, some for more than a decade.

"It feels like the end of the world," said Hla Phyo, who had been away from Myanmar for more than six years.

The men talked about conditions on the boats, the type of fish they caught and friends who had died in accidents or from illnesses. But I don't speak Burmese, and the interviews were conducted in broken Indonesian – not an ideal situation. Eddy stepped in with a suggestion.

"Well ... I could take you to the graveyard," he said. "There are a lot of Burmese guys there."

The blue, white and green burial markers were visible even from his boat. There were more than 60 in total, some broken or overrun by jungle weeds and trees. Each was inscribed with a Thai name, birth date, address and the ship on which they worked. But it was all a lie, Eddy and others there said. Many of the men buried in those graves were Burmese slaves, forced to be identified by the fake identities on their seafarer books even in death.

Grave markers are show where foreign fishing boat crew members who died on their ships are buried in Benjina, November 23, 2014. (AP Photo/Dita Alangkara)

It was an unbelievable turn, and left me enraged. I climbed a hill behind the fishing company, the only place where the signal was strong enough to send a phone text message to Mason: "You aren't going to believe this!"

After several days and nights on the island, Alangkara and Syam, both from the Jakarta bureau, had been getting their own evidence. Before we arrived on Benjina, a source had given us a grainy picture of a company jail that apparently was being used to keep men from running away. Alangkara and Syam managed to grab a few covert shots of eight men in the cage.

They also documented boats being loaded and unloaded with slave-caught fish, and broke away from their minders to film the graveyard.

But local authorities were soon onto them. Worried they might lose their footage, they decided to go, leaving me behind with a plan: Bring in reporter Esther Htusan, a native Burmese speaker, from Yangon to help.

With her arrival in Benjina, the language barrier was lifted and the doors swung wide open for us.

AP reporter Esther Htusan

Using a handheld video camera, we interviewed as many men as we could, more than 40 in total. Htusan also gave the camera to a dockworker, a slave himself, so he could get a quick interview with one of the men in the cage. From behind the rusty bars, he looked straight into the lens – just out of sight of a security guard – and said he and the others were locked up because they were considered flight risks. Their only crime was asking to go home.

That same evening, we filmed men on a slave ship as it came into dock. Two men were standing at the rail, smoking cigarettes, backlit by the fluorescent light on deck.

"Are you Burmese?" she yelled to them from a small boat, camera rolling. At first, they didn't know what to make of her and joked around. But she shouted for them to take her seriously: She was a journalist with an American news agency there to record their stories. Other men started arriving. Soon there were four, then six, eight and finally 12. Showing tremendous courage, with their captain just on the other side of the ship, the men jostled to be heard.

These rare, powerful images of captive slaves begging to be rescued would eventually lead both the text story and AP's television piece.

The desperation on Benjina was everywhere. Few men had been able to reach their families by phone, so they poured out of brothels to talk to Htusan, begging her to help them get messages to their families back in Myanmar.

We'd successfully avoided company officials, security guards and site managers for days, but knew they were finally on to us. And they had had enough.

"This is private property,"Htusan and I were told after several stern warnings. "Don't let us see you here again!"

On our last night in Benjina, we asked a boatman to take us across the channel one last time to get footage of slaves loading freshly caught seafood onto a 3,000-ton refrigerated Thai cargo ship. But this time, the company was ready. Two hired thugs from the ship jumped into a waiting speedboat and raced after us, coming within a few meters of ramming our small wooden boat. The pursuers backed off at the last minute when they saw my Western face. But their message had been delivered.

"It felt like my soul left my body," said Htusan, holding up her trembling hands, knowing by now that threats of violence in the remote, lawless region had to be taken seriously.

At dawn the next morning, Htusan and I were safely off the island.

Following the fish: Mason and McDowell on surveillance

The next step in the investigation was proving where the fish ultimately ended up. Mason and McDowell describe the process:

We now had video and photographs of the slaves' seafood being loaded onto the Thai-owned Silver Sea Line cargo ship, so we used a marine satellite tracking service to follow it on a map with live transmissions of its current location and speed. For two weeks, we watched the ship's icon move across the screen, covering thousands of miles of ocean until finally arriving at the Thai port of Samut Sakhon, about an hour south of Bangkok.

We were there to watch it unload.

For the next four nights, we surreptitiously followed trucks delivering slave-caught seafood to processors, freezer warehouses and distributors, noting the names of the companies. It was anything but glamorous. We crammed into the back cab of a small pickup truck along with a photographer and a videographer, and were forced to stay inside for hours at a time to avoid being seen.

Two refrigerated cargo ships, the Silver Sea 2, background, and the Silver Sea Line, foreground, are docked at Thajeen Port in Samut Sakhon, Thailand, December 10 2014. (AP Photo/Wong Maye-E)

We had been warned repeatedly that the area wasn't safe. Thailand has long been a haven for human trafficking, fueled by corruption and crime, and this part of the country was controlled by a powerful fish mafia where disputes sometimes end in shootings.

Undaunted, we tailed truckload after truckload of the Benjina seafood, sometimes into the early hours of the morning. We drove on busy highways and turned down narrow streets, documenting everything we saw.

We didn't realize it then, but we were slowly peeling back the murky layers that have allowed slavery to flourish for years in the Thai fishing industry.

Slave-caught fish and U.S. tables: Mendoza makes the connection

Each small factory that accepted one of the loads of slave-caught fish raised the question, where does it go next? Pulitzer Prize-winning reporter Mendoza went to work. Her account:

AP reporter Martha Mendoza

We spent weeks calling distributors, processors, freezers, and visiting Thailand's largest fish market and talking to security guards and workers to obtain information that linked them to large Thai seafood export businesses.

In California, I began a search of my own, looking through U.S. Customs records to trace the seafood directly to companies familiar to most Americans.

Plugging away at databases that track U.S. imports, I checked to see whether the companies receiving the tainted fish in Thailand were shipping to a U.S. distributor, and whether those deliveries were packaged and branded.

It was relatively easy to determine that cans of cat food labeled Fancy Feast, Meow Mix and Iams came out of Thai processors that bought fish off the boat from Benjina. But the U.S. distributors were more complicated because they are not required to disclose where they sell fish. Thus began my odyssey to dozens of supermarkets in different states to check out frozen and canned seafood. Was it from Thailand? Was it a species we had seen? What brand was it? Who was the distributor? Then it was back to the databases for a potential match.

　　This became part of my daily life for weeks. I even took my husband on a date night to a local Wal-Mart to search for seafood. One day, driving home from my daughter's field trip, I pulled into another Wal-Mart, sending out an army of fifth-graders to examine bags of frozen fish and filling my iPhone with photos of labels. On weekends, Mason and I swapped snapshots as we grocery shopped, a continent away from one another.

Back label of a Publix brand shrimp cocktail platter, a product of Thailand, purchased in Orlando, Florida, November 16, 2015. (AP Photo/John Raoux)

　　Eventually, the puzzle came together. With weeks of database tracking, we found seafood from Benjina in the supply chains of supermarkets, distribution centers and restaurants in every state at thousands of outlets. And then, with a videographer and photographer, I headed to Boston for the North American Seafood Expo to talk to companies with tainted supply chains, industry groups and Thai and Indonesian representatives.

The National Fisheries Institute, in a pre-emptive strike, sent a warning to the companies at the show: "Prepare for major AP story on labor abuse in seafood: Association advises members Pulitzer Prize-winning journalist reporting from Boston show floor."

The warning had an impact. We were followed by men, apparently working for seafood firms, as we worked the floor. Salespeople turned their backs. When we were told to come back later, we simply sat down and waited, sometimes for hours.

Eventually we had given all the subjects of our story an opportunity to respond, and obtained comment on camera from Thai and Indonesian authorities. We were ready to publish.

But there was still one major obstacle left. The men on Benjina identified by name, in photos or in video were vulnerable. And we couldn't run the story until their safety was guaranteed.

On the wire: The final push

The AP went into high gear to get the story published, without endangering the men. Mason, Mendoza and McDowell consulted with Mary Rajkumar, international enterprise editor, and other top news leaders for a quick call: Everyone agreed that the men had to be rescued before publication. But how?

Mason knew how to get the answer. She took the video of enslaved men to a trusted source at the International Organization for Migration so he could see the power of the images for himself. He immediately understood the importance of the story and promised to do his best to help.

About two weeks before the story ran, Indonesia's marine police, with information from the IOM, rescued eight men from the island – including the man the AP had videotaped behind bars in the locked cage.

The story moved on March 24, 2015. Its impact was tremendous and immediate. Thai Union, a huge exporter to the U.S. highlighted in the story, announced the next day that they had fired a supplier. Seafood businesses were inundated with calls. Three U.S. groups representing retail and seafood businesses, including Wal-Mart and Whole Foods, wrote a letter to the Thai and Indonesian ambassadors in Washington to demand action.

AP International Enterprise Editor, Mary Rajkumar

"One of the problems we have faced in addressing these challenges is the lack of specificity of allegations," it said. "The AP article changes this dynamic."

The Thai military government at first threatened to crack down on all media reporting about abuses in the fishing industry, with the prime minister warning anyone who writes about it should be "executed." The government has since acknowledged the trafficking scourge and pledged to clean it up.

In the U.S., Mendoza attended a Congressional hearing and wrote about new legislation requiring large companies to disclose policies to keep their supply chains free of slavery.

But the biggest impact came in Indonesia itself. Just over a week after the story was published, the Indonesian government launched a fact-finding trip to several islands, including Benjina. Susi Pudjiastuti, the tough new fisheries minister, said AP's documentation finally gave her the proof she needed to act on the longstanding problem of human trafficking. Fed up with illegal fishing, which was costing the country billions, she had already ordered a moratorium on all foreign fishing vessels. This forced thousands of slaves onto land, where they could easily be interviewed and rescued.

Here's McDowell's account of the return to Benjina:

This time, we arrived on the island with government officials determined to see the situation for themselves. The results were breathtaking.

The men told the investigators the same stories about their brutal work and captivity on the island. In order to protect them from retribution, Indonesian authorities initially told about 20 men from Myanmar that could be moved for their safety. But as news spread that some men were getting to leave the island, dozens, then hundreds, of other men began arriving, pleading to leave.

"They can all come," one of the officials said. "We don't want to leave a single person behind."

Men started running to the port from the hills and jungle, sprinting to their boats to reclaim their meager belongings. They raised their hands in unison when officials asked who among them wanted to go home. For these men, their nightmare was finally ending.

Burmese fishermen run to collect their belongings after being informed that they can leave, at the compound of Pusaka Benjina Resources fishing company in Benjina, April 3, 2015. (AP Photo/Dita Alangkara)

Twenty-two years a slave: One man's story

After interviewing dozens of rescued slaves, Mason found one with an extraordinary story. She followed him from the island of Tual, Indonesia, where all of the freed slaves were temporarily housed, to his home in Myanmar. Here is her account:

I couldn't believe it when I met Myint Naing in Tual. He told me he had been in Indonesia since being trafficked in 1993 – the year I graduated high school.

Former slave fisherman Myint Naing, center, hugs his niece Kyi Wai Hnin, right, and nephew Kyaw Min Tun following his return to his village in Mon State, Myanmar, May 16, 2015. (AP Photo/Gemunu Amarasinghe)

He pulled back the hair on top of his head to show me a jagged scar, telling me his skull had been cracked by one of his bosses, simply for asking if he could go home. Later, he asked a second time, and was shackled to his boat with no food or water and told he would be killed. He managed to escape one night and swam to shore. He then hid in the jungle with help from a local family for years.

Myint boarded the first of four planes that took the former slaves back to Myanmar. When he arrived at the biggest city, Yangon, I was there with a team of AP reporters to meet him. We followed him as he boarded an overnight bus with other men from

Mon State, and then in a car that took him to the village he'd left behind 22 years ago.

As Myint leaped from the vehicle, we watched what could have been a scene from a movie. First, Myint embraced his sobbing baby sister. Then, a small, frail figure ran toward him. He wailed and then fell to the ground before he was pulled into his mother's arms.

Htusan and I hugged on the side of the road as we were overcome. This was the true power of journalism, and we all knew it was happening over and over in villages across Southeast Asia. It was amazing to see, but even more amazing because we helped make it happen.

The investigation continues: More to come

AP's work on the story is unfinished. The release of the first slaves was followed by a four-month quest, using satellites and sources, to find men the reporters knew were still enslaved at sea after their boats fled Benjina.

Nearly two years into the investigation, the impossible question has clearly been answered: thousands of enslaved men have been forced to fish, catching seafood that ends up on U.S. dinner tables. But much more remains to be done. The chance to make a difference is what led us to our profession in the first place, and with the support of the AP, further reporting is already underway.

Chapter 1

WHO CAUGHT THE FISH YOU BOUGHT?

Burmese fishermen slaves arrive at the compound of Pusaka Benjina fishing company to report for departure from Benjina, Aru Islands, Indonesia. Hundreds of foreign fishermen rushed at the chance to be rescued from the isolated island where an Associated Press report revealed slavery runs rampant in the industry. Indonesian officials investigating abuses offered to take them out of concern for the men's safety, April 3, 2015. (AP Photo/Dita Alangkara)

NO ESCAPE
Ambon, Indonesia, Saturday, June 14, 2014

He was too sick to eat, and Min Min Chan's chest ached with each breath he sucked. It didn't matter: The Thai captain warned him to get back on deck and start hauling fish onto the trawler or be tossed overboard. As a 17-year-old slave stuck in the middle of the sea, he knew no one would come looking if he simply vanished.

Less than a month earlier, Chan had left Myanmar for neighboring Thailand, looking for work. Instead, he said a broker tricked and sold him onto the fishing boat for $616. He ended up far away in Indonesian waters before even realizing what was happening.

Tens of thousands of invisible migrants like Chan stream into Thailand, Southeast Asia's second-largest economy, every year. Many are used as forced labor in various industries, especially on long-haul fishing boats that catch seafood eaten in the U.S. and around the world. Others are dragged into the country's booming sex industry. Ethnic Rohingya asylum seekers from neighboring Myanmar are also held for ransom in abysmal jungle camps.

Next week, when a U.S. report on human trafficking comes out, Thailand may be punished for allowing that exploitation. The country has been on a U.S. State Department human trafficking watch list for the past four years. Washington warned in last year's report that without major improvements, it would be dropped to the lowest rung, Tier 3, joining the ranks of North Korea, Syria, Iran and Zimbabwe.

Secretary of State John Kerry speaks during the release of the 2014 Trafficking in Persons Report at the State Department in Washington. Failure to meet minimum standards in fighting human trafficking has landed Thailand and Malaysia on a State Department blacklist, June 20, 2014. (AP Photo/Jose Luis Magana)

Though Thailand says it is trying to prevent such abuses and punish traffickers, its authorities have been part of the problem. The U.S. has said the involvement of corrupt officials appears to be widespread, from protecting brothels and workplaces to cooperating directly with traffickers.

A downgrade could lead the U.S. to pull back certain forms of foreign support and exchange programs as well as oppose assistance from international financial institutions such as the World Bank. Washington has already cut some assistance to Bangkok following last month's Thai military coup.

Thailand is paying a U.S. public relations company $51,000 a month to help in its push for better standing. The government issued a progress report for 2013, noting that investigations, prosecutions and the budget for anti-trafficking work all are on the rise.

"We recognize that it's a very serious, very significant problem, and we've been building a legal and bureaucratic framework to try to address these issues," said Vijavat Isarabhakdi, Thailand's ambassador to the U.S. "We feel that we have turned a corner and are making great progress in this area."

At least 38 Thai police were punished last year or are being investigated for alleged involvement in trafficking, but none has stood trial yet. Four companies have been fined, and criminal charges against five others are pending. But the government pulled the licenses of only two of the country's numerous labor recruitment agencies.

In Geneva on Wednesday, Thailand was the only government in the world to vote against a new U.N. international treaty that combats forced labor by, among other things, strengthening victims' access to compensation. Several countries abstained.

"Thailand tries to portray itself as the victim while, at the same time, it's busy taking advantage of everybody it can who's coming through the country," said Phil Robertson, deputy director of Human Rights Watch's Asia division. "The exploitation of migrants, the trafficking, it comes through Thailand because people know they can pay people in the government and in the police to look the other way."

Chan's story is a common nightmare. A recruiter showed up in his village in Myanmar, also known as Burma, offering good money to work on a fishing boat in Thailand. Chan said after sneaking across the border by foot, he was sold onto a boat by the broker and told to hide inside to avoid being seen by Thai authorities.

"'You have to work at least six months. After that, you can go back home,'" Chan said the captain told him. "I decided, 'I can work for six months on this boat.'"

But after the ship docked 17 days later on eastern Indonesia's Ambon island, Chan met other Burmese workers who told a very different story: There was no six-month contract and no escape. Now thousands of miles from home, he realized he no longer owned his life - it had become a debt that must be paid.

Ambon, Indonesia (AP)

Ambon, in the Banda Sea, is peppered with churches and pristine dive sites. At the port, deep-sea fishermen in tattered T-shirts and rubber boots form human chains on boats, tossing bag after bag of frozen snapper and other fish into pickup trucks bound for cold storage. Much of it will later be shipped to Thailand for export.

They speak Burmese, Thai and other languages. Their skin is dark from the sun, and some faces look far older than their ropey bodies.

On the cramped boat, Chan said he slept only about three hours a night alongside 17 other men, mostly Burmese, sometimes working on just one meal of rice and fish a day. There was no fresh water for drinking or bathing, only boiled sea water with a briny taste.

In his first month at sea, he got sick and didn't eat for three days. He was sleeping when the captain threatened him.

"Why are you not working? Why are you taking a rest?" Chan recalled him saying. "Do we have to throw you off into the water?"

Some of Chan's friends carried him onto the deck, where he was given medicine before getting back to work.

For the next year, he labored, hauling up thousands of kilograms (pounds) of fish as he tried to shake a stubborn cough. He saw land every couple of months, but there was no way to leave the port.

He said he was given occasional packs of cigarettes, noodles and coffee, but he never got paid.

Thailand shipped some $7 billion worth of seafood abroad last year, making it the world's third-largest exporter. Most went to Japan and the U.S., where it ranks as the No. 3 foreign supplier.

The United Nations estimates the industry employs 2 million people, but it still faces a massive worker shortage. Many Thais are unwilling to take the low-paid, dangerous jobs that can require fishermen to be at sea for months or even years at a time.

An estimated 200,000 migrants, mostly from neighboring Myanmar and Cambodia, are laboring on Thai boats, according to the Bangkok-based nonprofit Raks Thai Foundation. Some go voluntarily, but a U.N. survey last year of nearly 600 workers in the fishing industry found that almost none had a signed contract, and about 40 percent had wages cut without explanation. Children were also found on board.

Forced or coerced work is more common in certain sectors, including deep-sea fishing and seafood processing plants where some workers have reported being drugged and kidnapped.

Foreign fishermen sit on their boat anchored off the town of Ambon, Maluku province, Indonesia, September 9, 2015. (AP Photo/Achmad Ibrahim)

Long-haul fishermen like Chan have it the worst. They are worked around the clock seven days a week with very little food and often no clean water. They risk getting fouled in lines, being swept overboard during storms or losing fingers cleaning fish.

But often the biggest threat is their captain. A 2009 U.N. report found that about six out of 10 migrant workers on Thai fishing boats reported seeing a co-worker killed. Chan faced abuse himself and saw one sick Burmese fisherman die. The captain simply dumped the body overboard.

Thailand's progress report highlighted increased boat and workplace inspections, but the U.S. has said those do not combat trafficking in an industry where "overall impunity for exploitative labor practices" is seen. The U.S. recommends increased prosecutions of employers involved in human trafficking.

The problem is also rampant in the country's notorious sex industry. More than three-quarters of trafficking investigations launched last year in Thailand involved sexual exploitation. Thai girls and women were abused along with those from neighboring countries.

Another challenge surrounds the recent influx of Rohingya Muslims. An estimated 75,000 have fled Myanmar since communal violence exploded there two years ago, according to Chris Lewa of the nonprofit Arakan Project. The Buddhist-dominated country considers Rohingya to be noncitizens from Bangladesh, though many were born in Myanmar.

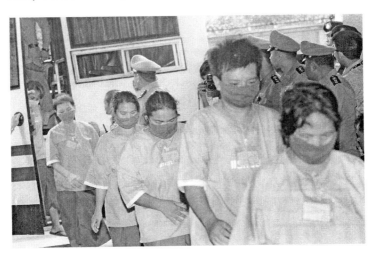

Female suspects allegedly involved in human trafficking of Rohingya migrants file into the Criminal Court in Bangkok, Thailand, November 10, 2015. (AP Photo/Sakchai Lalit)

Many Rohingya brought to Thailand are held at rubber plantations or forest camps by armed guards until they can find a way to pay the typical asking price of $2,000 for their release, according to victims and rights groups. Those who get the money often cross the border into Malaysia, where tens of thousands of Rohingya have found refuge. Those who don't are sometimes sold for sex, forced labor, or they are simply left to die.

The Thai government, however, does not address these asylum seekers as trafficking victims in its report. It said fleeing Rohingya enter Thailand willingly, even though "most of them fall prey to smugglers and illegal middlemen." However, Vijavat, the Thai ambassador, said some cases are now being treated as trafficking.

Rights groups allege corrupt Thai officials are sometimes involved, including deporting Rohingya straight back into traffickers' hands.

"I believe we have more good officers than bad ones," said police Col. Paisith Sungkahapong, director of the government's Anti-Human Trafficking Center. He said migrants in the country illegally "are pushed back through proper channels. Immigration will contact their counterpart in Myanmar or whichever country, and make sure they return there safely."

In a letter last month to U.S. Secretary of State John Kerry, a group of 18 human rights groups and labor organizations highlighted the Rohingya issue, while urging the U.S. government to put more pressure on Bangkok to crack down on the seafood industry and keep fish caught by slaves from ending up on American dinner tables.

"The (Thai) government continues to be at best complacent, at worst complicit, in the trafficking of migrant workers from neighboring countries to provide inexpensive labor for export industries," they wrote.

After a year on the boat, Chan finally started getting paid: about $87 every two months. He continued working for a total of three and a half years, until he started coughing blood and became too weak to continue.

When he asked the captain if he could go home, he was told to get back to work.

"I thought it was better to die by jumping into the water than to die by being tortured by these people," he said. "When I was about to jump, my friend grabbed me from the back and saved me."

His crew members instead convinced him to slip away the next time they made land, and he eventually escaped into Ambon where a local woman helped him get treatment for tuberculosis. After recovering, he decided to stay with her, and she treated him like a son. He worked odd jobs for the next four years, but never stopped dreaming of home.

Finally, at age 24, he found someone at Indonesia's immigration office willing to help. And in March, the International Organization for Migration arranged for him and 21 other trafficked Burmese fishermen to fly home.

Burmese trafficking victim Min Min Chan, center, sits with others in a bus that will take them to their transit hotel before returning to their country, at Soekarno-Hatta International Airport in Jakarta, Indonesia, March 11, 2014. (AP Photo/Dita Alangkara)

Hours before boarding the plane, Chan wondered what would be left of his old life when he landed. More than seven years had passed without a letter or a phone call. He had no idea if he would be able to find his family, or even if they were still alive.

"After I knew the broker sold me into slavery ... I felt so sad," he said. "When I left Myanmar, I had a great life."

OVERFISHING DRIVING SLAVERY
Samut Sakhon, Wednesday, February 25, 2015

Urine pools under a bed where an emaciated Burmese man lies wearing only a T-shirt and a diaper.

As he struggles to sit up and steady himself, he tears at his thick, dark hair in agitation. He cannot walk and doesn't remember his family or even his own name. He speaks mostly gibberish in broken Indonesian - a language he learned while working in the country as a slave aboard a Thai fishing boat.

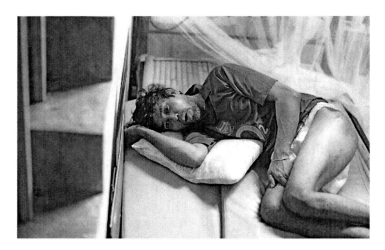

Min Min, a fisherman slave from Myanmar, rests on a make-shift bed. Min Min was res-cued from a tiny island two months ago, on the verge of starvation, and brought back to Thailand, December 12, 2014. (AP Photo/Wong Maye-E)

Near death from a lack of proper food, he was rescued from a tiny island in Indonesia two months ago. He is just one of countless hidden casualties from the fishing industry in Thailand, the world's third-largest seafood exporter.

A report released Wednesday by the British nonprofit Environmental Justice Foundation said that overfishing and the use of illegal and undocumented trawlers have ravaged Thailand's marine ecosystems and depleted fish stocks. Boats are now catching about 85 percent less than what they brought in 50 years ago, making it "one of the most overfished regions on the planet," the report said.

Shrinking fisheries in the Gulf of Thailand and Andaman Sea have, in turn, pushed Thai fishing boats farther and farther from home. The group estimates that up to half of all fish labeled a "product of Thailand" is sourced from outside its borders - mainly in Asia, but as far away as Africa.

The report, compiled from the group's own research and the work of others, explains how Thailand's vast seafood industry is al-most wholly dependent on cheap migrant labor. Since few Thais are willing to take the dangerous, low-level jobs that can take them far from home, a sophisticated network of brokers and agents has emerged, regularly recruiting laborers from impoverished neighboring countries such as Myanmar and Cambodia, often through trickery and kidnapping.

A Thai trawler is seen returning to port after a fishing trip in the waters of the Gulf of Thailand in Samut Sakhon Province, west of Bangkok, Thailand. The environmental and human rights group Environmental Justice Foundation has charged that Thailand is not adequately addressing severe abuse against Myanmar migrant workers in the Thai fishing industry. The British-based group said in its report entitled "Slavery at Sea" that the Thai government has failed to act strongly against human trafficking and that violence is routine in the industry, September 3, 2013. (AP Photo/Sakchai Lalit)

Men - and sometimes children as young as 13 - are sold onto boats where they typically work 18- to 20-hour days with little food and often only boiled sea water to drink, enduring beatings and sometimes even death at the hands in their captains. Most are paid little or nothing. They can be trapped at sea for months or years at a time; transshipment vessels are routinely used to pick up catches and deliver supplies.

Concerns about labor abuses, especially at sea, prompted the U.S. State Department last year to downgrade Thailand to the lowest level in its annual human trafficking report, putting the country on par with North Korea, Iran and Syria. It highlighted abuse on both ships and in processing plants, noting widespread involvement from corrupt officials.

The Southeast Asian nation responded by launching a major public relations campaign, with the government drafting its own country assessment to highlight steps taken to clean up the industry since a military junta took control of Thailand in May. The unreleased Thai report, obtained by The Associated Press, includes establishing a new national registry of illegal migrant workers and plans for stricter labor regulations on vessels and in the seafood industry.

However, just a month after the new government stepped in, Thailand was the only country in the world to vote against a U.N. international treaty aimed at stopping forced labor.

"If you drill down, if you look at the substance of enforcement and the implementation of existing laws and regulations, it's minimal," said Steve Trent, the group's executive director. "What the Thai government seems to do repeatedly, again and again in the face of these accusations, is conduct a high-powered PR exercise rather than seek to address the problem."

A Thai government spokesman and officials at the Department of Fisheries did not immediately respond to The Associated Press' requests for comment.

Thailand, which exported $7 billion in seafood in 2013, is one of the biggest suppliers to the U.S. But a study published last year in the journal Marine Policy estimated 25 percent to 40 percent of tuna shipped from Thailand to America is from illegal or unreported sources - the highest rate of any species or country examined - and is frequently linked to labor abuses at sea.

Human rights advocates say some improvements have been noted in domestic waters, but such policies have little impact when vessels stray into the territorial waters of other countries. Traveling longer distances to catch fish raises operating costs, and increases pressure on fishing companies to save money by relying on forced, bonded and slave labor.

"On long-haul boats, nothing has changed in the brutal working conditions and physical abuse meted out by captains against their crews," said Phil Robertson, deputy director of Human Rights Watch's Asia division, who has worked extensively on the issue. "The reality is the Thai government's high-sounding rhetoric to stop human trafficking and clean up the fishing fleets still largely stops at the water's edge."

Thai Frozen Foods Association President Dr. Poj Aramwattananont speaks during an interview at the Seafood Expo in Boston. He said Thais know that human trafficking is wrong, but Thai companies cannot always track down the origins of their fish and whether it is "good or bad", March 16, 2015. (AP Photo/Elise Amendola)

The man rescued from the Indonesian island in December now remembers his name - Min Min - and bits of his old life in Myanmar, also known as Burma. But his mind remains far from clear.

He knows he worked three years on a boat in Indonesia where his ankles were sometimes bound with rope. He recalls collapsing one day on deck during a storm and being unconscious for three hours before the Thai captain forced him to get up and haul the nets back in.

Eventually, he became too sick and weak to work and was abandoned on the remote island two years ago.

Min Min was on the verge of starvation when he was rescued and taken to the nonprofit Labor Rights Protection Network in Samut Sakhon, a gritty port town on the outskirts of Bangkok. He's eating well and taking vitamins to try to regain his strength, and he can now stand and slowly shuffle across the floor.

He is still far from well. He's confused about such basics as his age, saying once that he is 43 and later that he is 36. If his family back in Myanmar is mentioned, he becomes rattled and stutters his thoughts as if it's too much to bear.

"Working on the boat is no good. People like to take advantage of you," he said. "If I recover from my illness, I'll never be on a boat again in my life. Never again. I'm scared."

Chapter 2

BENJINA ISLAND

Kyaw Naing, a slave fisherman from Myanmar, talks to a security guard through the bars of a cell at the compound of a fishing company in Benjina, Indonesia, November 22, 2014. (AP Photo/Dita Alangkara)

LIVING IN A CAGE
Benjina, Indonesia, Wednesday, March 25, 2015

The Burmese slaves sat on the floor and stared through the rusty bars of their locked cage, hidden on a tiny tropical island thousands of miles from home.

Just a few yards away, other workers loaded cargo ships with slave-caught seafood that clouds the supply networks of major supermarkets, restaurants and even pet stores in the United States.

But the eight imprisoned men were considered flight risks - laborers who might dare run away. They lived on a few bites of rice and curry a day in a space barely big enough to lie down, stuck until the next trawler forces them back to sea.

Thai and Burmese fishing boat workers sit inside a cell at the compound of a fishing company in Benjina, Indonesia, November 22, 2014. (AP Photo/Dita Alangkara)

"All I did was tell my captain I couldn't take it anymore, that I wanted to go home," said Kyaw Naing, his dark eyes pleading into an Associated Press video camera sneaked in by a sympathetic worker. "The next time we docked," he said nervously out of earshot of a nearby guard, "I was locked up."

Here, in the Indonesian island village of Benjina and the surrounding waters, hundreds of trapped men represent one of the most desperate links criss-crossing between companies and countries in the seafood industry. This intricate web of connections separates the fish we eat from the men who catch it, and obscures a brutal truth: Your seafood may come from slaves.

The men the AP interviewed on Benjina were mostly from Myanmar, also known as Burma, one of the poorest countries in the world. They were brought to Indonesia through Thailand and forced to fish. Their catch was then shipped back to Thailand, where it entered the global stream of commerce.

Tainted fish can wind up in the supply chains of some of America's major grocery stores, such as Kroger, Albertsons and Safeway; the nation's largest retailer, Wal-Mart; and the biggest food distributor, Sysco. It can find its way into the supply chains of some of the most popular brands of canned pet food, including Fancy Feast, Meow Mix and Iams. It can turn up as calamari at fine dining restaurants, as imitation crab in a California sushi roll or as packages of frozen snapper relabeled with store brands that land on our dinner tables.

Foreign fishermen gather on their boat during an inspection conducted by Indonesian officials in Benjina, April 3, 2015. (AP Photo/Dita Alangkara)

In a year-long investigation, the AP talked to more than 40 current and former slaves in Benjina. The AP documented the journey of a single large shipment of slave-caught seafood from the Indonesian village, tracking it by satellite to a gritty Thai harbor. Upon its arrival, AP journalists followed trucks that loaded and drove the seafood over four nights to dozens of factories, cold storage plants and the country's biggest fish market.

The tainted seafood mixes in with other fish at a number of sites in Thailand, including processing plants. U.S. Customs records show that several of those Thai factories ship to America. They also sell to Europe and Asia, but the AP traced shipments to the U.S., where trade records are public.

Workers in Benjina load fish onto a cargo ship bound for Thailand. In its first report on trafficking around the world, the U.S. criticized Thailand as a hub for labor abuse. Yet 14 years later, seafood caught by slaves on Thai boats is still slipping into the supply chains of major American stores and supermarkets, November 22, 2014. (AP Photo/Dita Alangkara)

By this time, it is nearly impossible to tell where a specific fish caught by a slave ends up. However, entire supply chains are muddied, and money is trickling down the line to companies that benefit from slave labor.

The major corporations contacted would not speak on the record but issued statements that strongly condemned labor abuses. All said they were taking steps to prevent forced labor, such as working with human rights groups to hold subcontractors accountable.

Several independent seafood distributors who did comment described the costly and exhaustive steps taken to ensure their supplies are clean. They said the discovery of slaves underscores how hard it is to monitor what goes on halfway around the world.

Santa Monica Seafood, a large independent importer that sells to restaurants, markets and direct from its store, has been a leader in improving international fisheries, and sends buyers around the world to inspect vendors.

"The supply chain is quite cloudy, especially when it comes from offshore," said Logan Kock, vice president for responsible sourcing, who acknowledged that the industry recognizes and is working to address the problem. "Is it possible a little of this stuff is leaking through? Yeah, it is possible. We are all aware of it."

The slaves interviewed by the AP had no idea where the fish they caught was headed. They knew only that it was so valuable, they were not allowed to eat it.

Workers in Benjina, load fish onto a cargo ship bound for Thailand, November 22, 2014. (AP Photo/Dita Alangkara)

They said the captains on their fishing boats forced them to drink unclean water and work 20- to 22-hour shifts with no days off. Almost all said they were kicked, whipped with toxic stingray tails or otherwise beaten if they complained or tried to rest. They were paid little or nothing, as they hauled in heavy nets with squid, shrimp, snapper, grouper and other fish.

Some shouted for help over the deck of their trawler in the port to reporters, as bright fluorescent lights silhouetted their faces in the darkness.

"I want to go home. We all do," one man called out in Burmese, a cry repeated by others. The AP is not using the names of some men for their safety. "Our parents haven't heard from us for a long time. I'm sure they think we are dead."

Another glanced fearfully over his shoulder toward the captain's quarters, and then yelled: "It's torture. When we get beaten, we can't do anything back. ... I think our lives are in the hands of the Lord of Death."

In the worst cases, numerous men reported maimings or even deaths on their boats.

"If Americans and Europeans are eating this fish, they should remember us," said Hlaing Min, 30, a runaway slave from Benjina. "There must be a mountain of bones under the sea. ... The bones of the people could be an island, it's that many."

For Burmese slaves, Benjina is the end of the world.

Roughly 3,500 people live in the town that straddles two small islands separated by a five-minute boat ride. Part of the Maluku chain, formerly known as the Spice Islands, the area is about 400 miles north of Australia, and hosts small kangaroos and rare birds of paradise with dazzling bright feathers.

Benjina is impossible to reach by boat for several months of the year, when monsoon rains churn the Arafura Sea. It is further cut off by a lack of Internet access. Before a cell tower was finally installed last month, villagers would climb nearby hills each evening in the hope of finding a signal strong enough to send a text. An old landing strip has not been used in years.

The small harbor is occupied by Pusaka Benjina Resources, whose five-story office compound stands out and includes the cage with the slaves. The company is the only fishing operation on Benjina officially registered in Indonesia, and is listed as the owner of more than 90 trawlers. However, the captains are Thai, and the Indonesian government is reviewing to see if the boats are really Thai-owned. Pusaka Benjina did not respond to phone calls and a letter, and did not speak to a reporter who waited for two hours in the company's Jakarta office.

On the dock in Benjina, former slaves unload boats for food and pocket money. Many are men who were abandoned by their captains - sometimes five, 10 or even 20 years ago - and remain stranded.

In the deeply forested island interiors, new runaways forage for food and collect rainwater, living in constant fear of being found by hired slave catchers.

And just off a beach covered in sharp coral, a graveyard swallowed by the jungle entombs dozens of fishermen. They are buried under fake Thai names given to them when they were tricked or sold onto their ships, forever covering up evidence of their captors' abuse, their friends say.

A man uses a plastic sheet to cover himself from the rain near the graves of foreign fishing boat crew members who died on their ships, in Benjina, November 23, 2014. (AP Photo/Dita Alangkara)

"I always thought if there was an entrance there had to be an exit," said Tun Lin Maung, a slave abandoned on Benjina, as other men nodded or looked at the ground. "Now I know that's not true."

The Arafura Sea provides some of the world's richest and most diverse fishing grounds, teeming with mackerel, tuna, squid and many other species.

Although it is Indonesian territory, it draws many illegal fishing fleets, including from Thailand. The trade that results affects the United States and other countries.

The U.S. counts Thailand as one of its top seafood suppliers, and buys about 20 percent of the country's $7 billion annual exports in the industry. Last year, the State Department blacklisted Thailand for failing to meet minimum standards in fighting human trafficking, placing the country in the ranks of North Korea, Syria and Iran. However, there were no additional sanctions.

Thailand's seafood industry is largely run off the backs of migrant laborers, said Kendra Krieder, a State Department analyst who focuses on supply chains. The treatment of some of these workers falls under the U.S. government's definition of slavery, which includes forcing people to keep working even if they once signed up for the jobs, or trafficking them into situations where they are exploited.

"In the most extreme cases, you're talking about someone kidnapped or tricked into working on a boat, physically beaten, chained," said Krieder. "These situations would be called modern slavery by any measure."

A security guard talks to detainees inside a cell at the compound of a fishing company in Benjina. The imprisoned men were considered slaves who might run away, November 22, 2014. (AP Photo/Dita Alangkara)

The Thai government says it is cleaning up the problem. On the bustling floor of North America's largest seafood show in Boston earlier this month, an official for the Department of Fisheries laid out a plan to address labor abuse, including new laws that mandate

wages, sick leave and shifts of no more than 14 hours. However, Ka-
monpan Awaiwanont stopped short when presented details about
the men in Benjina.

"This is still happening now?" he asked. He paused. "We are
trying to solve it. This is ongoing."

The Thai government also promises a new national registry of
illegal migrant workers, including more than 100,000 flooding the
seafood industry. However, policing has now become even harder
because decades of illegal fishing have depleted stocks close to
home, pushing the boats farther and deeper into foreign waters.

The Indonesian government has called a temporary ban on
most fishing, aiming to clear out foreign poachers who take billions
of dollars of seafood from the country's waters. As a result, more
than 50 boats are now docked in Benjina, leaving up to 1,000 more
slaves stranded onshore and waiting to see what will happen next.

Indonesian officials are trying to enforce laws that ban cargo
ships from picking up fish from boats at sea. This practice forces
men to stay on the water for months or sometimes years at a time,
essentially creating floating prisons.

Susi Pudjiastuti, the new Fisheries Minister, said she has heard
of different fishing companies putting men in cells. She added that
she believes the trawlers on Benjina may really have Thai owners,
despite the Indonesian paperwork, reflecting a common practice of
faking or duplicating licenses.

She said she is deeply disturbed about the abuse on Benjina
and other islands.

"I'm very sad. I lose my eating appetite. I lose my sleep," she
said. "They are building up an empire on slavery, on stealing, on
fish(ing) out, on massive environmental destruction for a plate of
seafood."

The story of slavery in the Thai seafood industry started decades ago with the same push-and-pull that shapes economic
immigration worldwide - the hope of escaping grinding poverty to
find a better life somewhere else.

In recent years, as the export business has expanded, it has become more difficult to convince young Burmese or Cambodian
migrants and impoverished Thais - all of whom were found on Benjina - to accept the dangerous jobs. Agents have become more
desperate and ruthless, recruiting children and the disabled, lying

about wages and even drugging and kidnapping migrants, according to a former broker who spoke on condition of anonymity to avoid retribution.

Indonesian Maritime and Fisheries Minister Susi Pudjiastuti, center, adjusts her sunglasses as she prepares for a photo session after the inauguration ceremony for the newly appointed Cabinet members at the presidential palace in Jakarta, Indonesia, October 27, 2014. (AP Photo/Dita Alangkara)

The broker said agents then sell the slaves, usually to Thai captains of fishing boats or the companies that own them. Each slave typically costs around $1,000, according to Patima Tungpuchayakul, manager of the Thai-based nonprofit Labor Rights Promotion Network Foundation. The men are later told they have to work off the "debt" with wages that don't come for months or years, or at all.

"The employers are probably more worried about the fish than the workers' lives," she said. "They get a lot of money from this type of business."

Illegal Thai boats are falsely registered to fish in Indonesia through graft, sometimes with the help of government authorities. Praporn Ekouru, a Thai former member of Parliament, admitted to the AP that he had bribed Indonesian officials to go into their waters, and complained that the Indonesian government's crackdown is hurting business.

"In the past, we sent Thai boats to fish in Indonesian waters by changing their flags," said Praporn, who is also chairman of the Songkhla Fisheries Association in southern Thailand. "We had to pay bribes of millions of baht per year, or about 200,000 baht ($6,100) per month. ... The officials are not receiving money anymore because this order came from the government."

Illegal workers are given false documents, because Thai boats cannot hire undocumented crew. One of the slaves in Benjina, Maung Soe, said he was given a fake seafarer book belonging to a Thai national, accepted in Indonesia as an informal travel permit. He rushed back to his boat to dig up a crinkled copy.

"That's not my name, not my signature," he said angrily, pointing at the worn piece of paper. "The only thing on here that is real is my photograph."

Soe said he had agreed to work on a fishing boat only if it stayed in Thai waters, because he had heard Indonesia was a place from which workers never came back.

"They tricked me," he said. "They lied to me. ... They created fake papers and put me on the boat, and now here I am in Indonesia."

The slaves said the level of abuse on the fishing boats depends on individual captains and assistants. Aung Naing Win, who left a wife and two children behind in Myanmar two years ago, said some fishermen were so depressed that they simply threw themselves into the water. Win, 40, said his most painful task was working without proper clothing in the ship's giant freezer, where temperatures drop to 39 degrees below zero.

"It was so cold, our hands were burning," he said. "No one really cared if anyone died."

The shipment the AP tracked from the port of Benjina carried fish from smaller trawlers; AP journalists talked to slaves on more than a dozen of them.

A crane hoisted the seafood onto a refrigerated cargo ship called the Silver Sea Line, with an immense hold as big as 50 semi-trucks. At this point, by United Nations and U.S. standards, every fish in that hold is considered associated with slavery.

The ship belongs to the Silver Sea Reefer Co., which is registered in Thailand and has at least nine refrigerated cargo boats. The company said it is not involved with the fishermen.

"We only carry the shipment and we are hired in general by clients," said owner Panya Luangsomboon. "We're separated from the fishing boats."

Frozen seafood is off-loaded from a refrigerated cargo ship called the Silver Sea Line, a 3,000-ton cargo ship, at Thajeen Port in Samut Sakhon, Thailand, December 11, 2014. (AP Photo/Wong Maye-E)

The AP followed the Silver Sea Line by satellite over 15 days to Samut Sakhon. When it arrived, workers on the dock packed the seafood over four nights onto more than 150 trucks, which then delivered their loads around the city.

One truck bore the name and bird logo of Kingfisher Holdings Ltd., which supplies frozen and canned seafood around the world. Another truck went to Mahachai Marine Foods Co., a cold storage business that also supplies to Kingfisher and other exporters, according to Kawin Ngernanek, whose family runs it.

"Yes, yes, yes, yes," said Kawin, who also serves as spokesman for the Thai Overseas Fisheries Association. "Kingfisher buys several types of products."

When asked about abusive labor practices, Kingfisher did not answer repeated requests for comment. Mahachai manager Narongdet Prasertsri responded, "I have no idea about it at all."

Every month, Kingfisher and its subsidiary KF Foods Ltd. sends about 100 metric tons of seafood from Thailand to America, according to U.S. Customs Bills of Lading. These shipments have gone to Santa Monica Seafood, Stavis Seafoods - located on Boston's historic Fish Pier - and other distributors.

The Stavis Seafoods booth at the Seafood Expo in Boston. Stavis prides itself on its responsible sourcing practices, March 16, 2015. (AP Photo/Elise Amendola)

Richard Stavis, whose grandfather started the dealership in 1929, shook his head when told about the slaves whose catch may end up at businesses he buys from. He said his company visits processors and fisheries, requires notarized certification of legal practices and uses third-party audits.

"The truth is, these are the kind of things that keep you up at night," he said. "That's the sort of thing I want to stop. ... There are companies like ours that care and are working as hard as they can."

Wholesalers like Stavis sell packages of fish, branded and unbranded, that can end up on supermarket shelves with a private label or house brand. Stavis' customers also include Sysco, the largest food distributor in the U.S.; there is no clear way to know which particular fish was sold to them.

Sysco declined an interview, but the company's code of conduct says it "will not knowingly work with any supplier that uses forced, bonded, indentured or slave labor."

Gavin Gibbons, a spokesman for National Fisheries Institute, which represents about 75 percent of the U.S. seafood industry, said the reports of abuse were "disturbing" and "disheartening." "But these type of things flourish in the shadows," he said.

A refrigerated truck enters the Thajeen Port where cargo ships carrying seafood are docked in Samut Sakhon, Thailand. It is in this port that slave-caught seafood starts to lose its history, December 10, 2014. (AP Photo/Wong Maye-E)

A similar pattern repeats itself with other shipments and other companies, as the supply chain splinters off in many directions in Samut Sakhon. It is in this Thai port that slave-caught seafood starts to lose its history.

The AP followed another truck to Niwat Co., which sells to Thai Union Manufacturing Co., according to part owner Prasert Luang-somboon. Weeks later, when confronted about forced labor in their supply chain, Niwat referred several requests for comment to Lu-angsomboon, who could not be reached for further comment.

Thai Union Manufacturing is a subsidiary of Thai Union Fro-zen Products PCL., the country's largest seafood corporation, with $3.5 billion in annual sales. This parent company, known simply as Thai Union, owns Chicken of the Sea and is buying Bumble Bee, although the AP did not observe any tuna fisheries. In September, it became the country's first business to be certified by Dow Jones for sustainable practices, after meeting environmental and social reviews.

President and CEO of Thai Union Group, Thiraphong Chansiri gestures during an interview at his company offices in Bangkok, Thailand, December 15, 2015. (AP Photo/Mark Baker)

Thai Union said it condemns human rights violations, but multiple stakeholders must be part of the solution. "We all have to admit that it is difficult to ensure the Thai seafood industry's supply chain is 100 percent clean," CEO Thiraphong Chansiri said in an emailed statement.

Thai Union ships thousands of cans of cat food to the U.S., including household brands like Fancy Feast, Meow Mix and Iams. These end up on shelves of major grocery chains, such as Kroger, Safeway and Albertsons, as well as pet stores; again, however, it's impossible to tell if a particular can of cat food might have slave-caught fish.

Fancy Feast cat food, fish and shrimp feast flavor, a product of Thailand, purchased at a Publix market in Orlando, Florida. A report commissioned by Nestle SA found that impoverished migrant workers in Thailand are sold or lured by false promises and forced to catch and process fish that ends up in the global food giant's supply chains. Nestle is not a major purchaser of seafood in Southeast Asia but does some business in Thailand, primarily for its Purina brand Fancy Feast cat food, November 16, 2015. (AP Photo/John Raoux)

Thai Union says its direct clients include Wal-Mart, which declined an interview but said in an email statement: "We care about the men and women in our supply chain, and we are concerned about the ethical recruitment of workers."

Wal-Mart described its work with several non-profits to end forced labor in Thailand, including Project Issara, and referred the AP to Lisa Rende Taylor, its director. She noted that slave-caught seafood can slip into supply chains undetected at several points, such as when it is traded between boats or mingles with clean fish at processing plants. She also confirmed that seafood sold at the Talay Thai market - to where the AP followed several trucks - can enter international supply chains.

"Transactions throughout Thai seafood supply chains are often not well-documented, making it difficult to estimate exactly how much seafood available on supermarket shelves around the world is tainted by human trafficking and forced labor," she said.

Poj Aramwattananont, president of an industry group that represents Thai Union, Kingfisher and others, said Thais are not "jungle people" and know that human trafficking is wrong. However, he acknowledged that Thai companies cannot always track down the origins of their fish.

"We don't know where the fish come from when we buy from Indonesia," said Poj of the Thai Frozen Foods Association. "We have no record. We don't know if that fish is good or bad."

The seafood the slaves on Benjina catch may travel around the world, but their own lives often end right here, in this island village.

A crude cemetery holds more than graves strangled by tall grasses and jungle vines, where small wooden markers are neatly labelled, some with the falsified names of slaves and boats. Only their friends remember where they were laid to rest.

A Thai official takes pictures of the graves of foreign fishermen at a cemetery in Benjina, April 1, 2015. (AP Photo/Dita Alangkara)

In the past, former slave Hla Phyo said, supervisors on ships simply tossed bodies into the sea to be devoured by sharks. But after authorities and companies started demanding that every man be accounted for on the roster upon return, captains began stowing corpses alongside the fish in ship freezers until they arrived back in Benjina, the slaves said.

Lifting his knees as he stepped over the thick brush, Phyo searched for two grave markers overrun by weeds - friends he helped bury.

It's been five years since he himself escaped the sea and struggled to survive on the island. Every night, his mind drifts back to his mother in Myanmar. He knows she must be getting old now, and he desperately wants to return to her. Standing among so many anonymous tombs stacked on top of each other, hopelessness overwhelms him.

"I'm starting to feel like I will be in Indonesia forever," he said, wiping a tear away. "I remember thinking when I was digging, the only thing that awaits us here is death."

Chapter 3

22 YEARS AS A SLAVE

Former slave fisherman Myint Naing, 40, left, is embraced by his mother Khin Than, second left, as his sister Mawli Than, right, is overcome with emotion after they were reunited after 22 years in their village in Mon State, Myanmar, May 16, 2015. (AP Photo/Gemunu Amarasinghe)

HE JUST WANTED TO GO HOME
Tual, Indonesia, Wednesday, June 30, 2015

All he did was ask to go home.

The last time the Burmese slave made the same request, he was beaten almost to death. But after being gone eight years and forced to work on a boat in faraway Indonesia, Myint Naing was willing to risk everything to see his mother again. His nights were filled with dreams of her, and time was slowly stealing her face from his memory.

So he threw himself on the ground and roped his arms around the captain's legs to beg for freedom.

The Thai skipper barked loud enough for all to hear that Myint would be killed for trying to abandon ship. Then he flung the fisherman onto the deck and chained down his arms and legs.

Myint was left for three days to burn in the searing sun and shiver in the nighttime rain, without food or water. He wondered how he would be killed. Would they throw his body overboard to wash up on shore, like the other corpses he'd seen? Would they shoot him? Or would they simply bash his head open, as they had done before?

He was never going to see his mother again. He would simply disappear, and she wouldn't even know where to look.

Every year, thousands of migrant workers like Myint are tricked or sold into the seafood industry's gritty underworld. It's a brutal trade that has operated for decades as an open secret in Southeast Asia's waters, where unscrupulous companies rely on slaves to supply fish to major supermarkets and stores worldwide.

Migrant workers from Myanmar clean fishing nets aboard a trawler after a fishing trip in the Gulf of Thailand in Samut Sakhon Province, west of Bangkok, Thailand, September 3, 2013. (AP Photo/Sakchai Lalit)

As part of a year-long investigation into the multibillion-dollar business, The Associated Press interviewed more than 340 current and former slaves, in person or in writing. The stories told by one after another are strikingly similar.

Myint is a thin, soft-spoken man with the wiry strength of someone who has worked hard all his life. Illness has left his right arm partly paralyzed and his mouth clenched into a forced half-smile. But when he breaks into laughter, you see flashes of the boy he once was, despite all that has happened in between - a 22-year odyssey recounted by Myint and his relatives.

He comes from a small village off a narrow, dusty road in southern Myanmar's Mon State, the oldest of four boys and two girls. In 1990, his father drowned while fishing, leaving him as the man in charge at just 15. He helped cook, wash clothes and care for his siblings, but they kept sliding deeper into poverty.

So when a fast-talking broker visited the neighborhood three years later with stories of jobs in Thailand, Myint was easily wooed. The agent offered $300 for just a few months of work - enough for some families to survive on for a year. He and several other young men quickly put their hands up to go.

His mother, Khin Than, wasn't so sure. He was only 18 years old, with no education or travel experience. But he kept begging, arguing that he wouldn't be gone long and relatives already working there could look after him.

Finally, she relented.

Neither of them knew it but, at that moment, Myint began a journey that would take him thousands of miles away from his family. He would miss births, deaths, marriages and the unlikely transition of his country from a dictatorship to a bumpy democracy. He would run away twice from the ruthless forced labor on a fishing boat, only to realize that he could never escape from the shadow of fear.

Yet on the day he left home in 1993, all Myint saw was promise. The broker hustled his new recruits to grab their bags immediately, and Myint's 10-year-old sister wiped tears from her cheeks as she watched him walk down the dirt track away from their village.

His mother wasn't home. He never got to say goodbye.

Thailand earns $7 billion a year from a seafood industry that runs on labor from the poorest parts of the country, along with Cambodia, Laos and especially Myanmar, otherwise known as Burma. Up to 200,000 estimated migrants, most of them illegal, work at sea. Their catch ends up halfway around the globe in the United States, Europe and Japan - on dinner tables and in cat food bowls.

As overfishing decimates stocks near Thailand's shores, trawlers have been forced to venture farther and farther into more plentiful foreign waters. The dangerous work keeps men at sea for months or even years with fake Thai identity documents, trapped aboard floating prisons run by captains with impunity. Though Thai officials deny it, they have long been accused of turning a blind eye to such practices.

After easily skirting police at the border with Thailand and being held in a small shed with little food for more than a month, Myint was shoved onto a boat. The men were at sea for 15 days and finally docked in the far eastern corner of Indonesia. The captain shouted that everyone on board now belonged to him, using words Myint would never forget:

"You Burmese are never going home. You were sold, and no one is ever coming to rescue you."

He was panicked and confused. He thought he would be fishing in Thai waters for only a few months. Instead the boys were taken to the Indonesian island of Tual in the Arafura Sea, one of the world's richest fishing grounds, stocked with tuna, mackerel, squid, shrimp and other lucrative species for export.

Myint spent weeks at a time on the open ocean, living only on rice and the parts of the catch no one else would eat. During the busiest times, the men worked up to 24 hours a day, hoisting heavy nets rippling with fish. They were forced to drink foul-tasting boiled sea water.

He was paid only $10 a month, and sometimes not at all. There was no medicine. Anyone who took a break or fell ill was beaten by the Thai captain, who once lobbed a piece of wood at Myint for not moving fish fast enough.

Nearly half the Burmese men surveyed by the AP said they were beaten, or witnessed others being abused. They were made to work almost nonstop for nearly no pay, with little food and unclean water. They were whipped with toxic stingray tails, shocked with Taser-like devices and locked in a cage for taking breaks or attempting to flee. Sometimes, the men said, the bodies of those who died were stashed in the ship's freezer alongside the fish.

Workers on some boats were killed for slowing down or trying to jump ship. The Burmese fishermen said others flung themselves overboard because they saw no escape. Myint spotted several bloated bodies floating in the water.

By 1996, after three years, he had had enough. Penniless and homesick, he waited until his boat returned to Tual. Then he went into the office on the dock and, for the first time, asked to go home.

His request was answered by a helmet cracking his skull. As blood oozed out, he used both hands to hold the wound together. The Thai man who hit him repeated the words that already haunted him:

"We will never let you Burmese fishermen go. Even when you die."

That was the first time he ran away.

On islands scattered throughout the Maluku chain in Indonesia, also known as the Spice Islands, thousands of migrant fishermen who have escaped or been abandoned by their captains quietly hide out in the jungle. Some start families with local women, partly to protect themselves from slave catchers. It's risky, but one of the only ways to find a semblance of freedom.

An Indonesian family took mercy on Myint until he healed, and then offered him food and shelter in exchange for work on their farm. For five years, he lived this simple life and tried to erase memories of the horrors at sea. He learned to speak the Indonesian language fluently and acquired a taste for the food, even though it was much sweeter than the salty Burmese dishes his mother fixed.

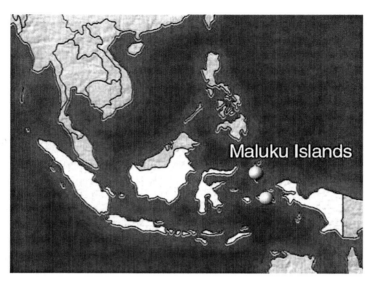

Indonesia map with Maluku Islands (AP)

But he couldn't forget his relatives in Myanmar or the friends he left behind on the boat. What happened to them? Were they still alive?

Sometimes Myint quietly visited other runaway Burmese slaves on the island to talk about home, bringing a big bag of vegetables he grew himself.

"He was a bit afraid to go around," remembered Naing Oo, another former Burmese slave in Tual. "It was very brutal on the fishing boats."

In the meantime, the world around him was changing. By 1998, Indonesia's longtime dictator Suharto had fallen, and the country was moving toward democracy. Myint wondered if maybe things were getting better on the ships too.

In 2001, he heard one captain was offering to take fishermen back to Myanmar if they agreed to work. He was determined to find a way home. So, eight years after he first arrived in Indonesia, he returned to the sea.

Right away, he knew he'd fallen into the same trap again. The work and conditions were just as appalling as the first time, and the money still didn't come.

If anything, the slavery was getting worse. Thailand was rapidly becoming one of the world's biggest seafood exporters, and needed more cheap labor. Brokers deceived, coerced or sometimes even drugged and kidnapped migrant workers, including children, the sick and the disabled.

After nine months on the water, Myint's captain broke his promise and told the crew he was abandoning them to go back to Thailand alone.

Furious and desperate, the Burmese slave once again pleaded to go home. That, he said, was when the captain chained him to the boat for three days.

Myint searched wildly for something, anything, to open the lock. Working it with his fingers was useless. Then he managed to fashion a small piece of metal into a makeshift pick and spent hours trying to quickly and quietly unlatch freedom. Finally, there was a click. The shackles slid off. He knew there wasn't much time, and if he got caught, death would come swiftly.

Sometime after midnight, he dove into the black water and swam to shore. Then he ran without looking back, in clothes still weighted by sea water.

He knew he had to disappear. This time, for good.

The slave trade in the Southeast Asian seafood industry is remarkable in its resilience. Over the past decade, outsiders have begun to take notice, and the U.S. government slams Thailand in annual reports year after year for pervasive labor abuses in fishing. Yet it continues, and it seldom lets go of the lives of those it ruins.

After he ran the second time, Myint hid alone in a bamboo shack in the jungle. But just three years later, he fell ill with what appeared to be a stroke. His nerves seemed to stop firing properly, leaving him easily chilled despite the oppressive tropical heat.

When he became too sick to work, the same Indonesian family cared for him with a kindness that reminded him of relatives back home. He had forgotten what his mother looked like, and knew that by now his favorite little sister would be all grown up. They likely thought he was dead.

What he didn't know was that his mother was like him: She never gave up. She prayed for him every day at the little Buddhist altar in her family's traditional stilt house, and asked fortune tellers year after year about her son. They assured her he was alive, but in a faraway place difficult to leave.

At one point, another Burmese man told the family that Myint was fishing in Indonesia and married. But Myint never wanted to be tethered to the country that had destroyed his life.

"I didn't want an Indonesian wife, I just wanted to go back home to Myanmar," he said. "I felt like I lost my young man's life. I just thought that all of this time, I should have been in Burma having a wife and a proper family."

After eight more years in the jungle without a clock or calendar, time began to blur. Now in his 30s, he started to believe the captain had been right: There really was no escape.

He couldn't go to the police or local officials, afraid they might hand him over to the captains for a fee. He had no way to call home. And he was scared to contact the Myanmar embassy because it would expose him as an illegal migrant.

In 2011, the solitude had become too much. Myint moved to the island of Dobo, where he had heard there were more Burmese. He and two other runaway slaves farmed chilies, eggplant, peas and beans until the police arrested one in the market and put him back on a boat. The man later fell sick at sea and died.

It was yet another reminder to Myint that if he wanted to survive, he needed to do it carefully.

One day in April, a friend came to him with news: An AP report linking slavery in the seafood industry to some of the biggest American grocery stores and pet food companies had spurred the Indonesian government to start rescuing current and former slaves on the islands. To date, more than 800 have been found and repatriated.

This was his chance. When the officials came to Dobo, he went back with them to Tual, where he was once a slave - this time to join hundreds of other free men.

After 22 years in Indonesia, Myint was finally going home. But what, he wondered, would he find?

Myint Naing waves as he carries his bag at a bus station in Yangon, Myanmar, on the journey home to Mon State. He is the oldest of four boys and two girls, May 15, 2015. (AP Photo/Gemunu Amarasinghe)

The flight from Indonesia to Myanmar's biggest city, Yangon, was a terrifying first for Myint. He walked out of the airport with a small black suitcase and a donated hat and shirt - all he had to show for his long time abroad.

Myint was coming back a stranger to his own country. Myanmar was no longer ruled by a secretive military government, and opposition leader Aung San Suu Kyi was free from years of house arrest and in Parliament.

The currency was baffling. He struggled to convert 15,000 Indonesian rupiah into about 1,000 Myanmar kyat, both roughly $1.

"I feel like a tourist," he said, sweat dripping down his face and chest. "I feel Indonesian."

The food was different, and so were the greetings. Myint kept shaking hands and touching his heart the Indonesian way, instead of bowing with his hands in a prayer position like a Burmese.

Even the words seemed odd. While he waited with other former slaves for the bus to Mon State, they chatted not in their native Burmese, but in Bahasa Indonesia.

"I don't want to speak that language anymore because I suffered so much there," he said. "I hate that language now." Yet he continued to slip in and out of it.

Myint Naing, 40, rear center, is seated on a bus with other former slave fisherman in Yangon, Myanmar, as they make their journey home to Mon State, May 15, 2015. (AP Photo/Gemunu Amarasinghe)

Most of all, just as the country had changed, so had he. He had left as a boy, but was returning a 40-year-old man who had been enslaved or in hiding for more than half his life. And he was the only one from his village to come back at all.

When he reached his home state, Myint's emotions started to fray. He was too nervous to eat. He fidgeted, running his hands through his hair and constantly rubbing the heart-shaped abalone pendant around his neck. Finally, it all became too much, and he started to sob.

"My life was just so bad that it hurts me a lot to think about it," he choked out. "I miss my mom."

He wondered if he would even recognize his mother and sister, or if they would remember him.

An hour later, he slapped his head in frustration as he tried to remember which way to go. The roads were now paved and lined with new buildings. He rubbed his palms on his pants and squirmed in excitement when he recognized a police station. He knew he was close.

Finally, the car he was riding in turned into a small village. He called a phone number that he had gotten only the day before. Seconds later, when he saw a plump Burmese woman - on the same road that had led him away so many years ago - he knew immediately it was his little sister.

They exploded into an embrace, and the tears that spilled were of joy and mourning for all the lost time apart. "Brother, it's so good that you are back!" she sobbed. "We don't need money! We just need family! Now you are back, it's all that we need."

Myint Naing, center, and his sister Mawli Than, left, embrace as they are reunited after 22 years at their village in Mon State, Myanmar, May 16, 2015. (AP Photo/Gemunu Amarasinghe)

But his mother was missing. Myint anxiously scanned the road as his sister frantically dialed a number.

And then a small, frail figure with gray-streaked hair began to run.

When he spotted her, he howled and fell to the ground, burying his face in his hands. She swept him up in her arms and softly stroked his head, cradling him as he let everything go.

Myint Naing and his mother, Khin Than, cry as they are reunited after 22 years at their village, May 16, 2015. (AP Photo/Gemunu Amarasinghe)

They wailed and wept so loudly, the whole village emerged to see what seemed like a ghost. "That guy's been gone for 20 years," one man said.

Myint, his mother and his sister walked arm-in-arm to the simple stilt house of his childhood. At the front gate, he crouched on his knees, and they heaved water with a traditional tamarind soap on his head to cleanse away evil spirits.

As his sister helped wash his hair, his 60-year-old mother turned pale and collapsed against a bamboo ladder. Then, suddenly, she grabbed her heart and began to gasp for air. Relatives and neighbors fanned her and fetched water and a lime to smell, but her eyes rolled back into her head. Someone yelled that she wasn't breathing.

Myint ran to her, dripping wet, and blew three breaths into her mouth.

"Open your eyes! Open your eyes!" he screamed, beating his chest with both hands. "I'll look after you from now on! I will make you happy! I don't want to see you sick! I am back home!"

Khin Than, center, is attended to after she fainted during a reunion with her son Myint Naing, May 16, 2015. (AP Photo/Gemunu Amarasinghe)

She slowly revived, and Myint took a long look into her eyes.

He was finally free to see the face from his dreams. He would never forget it again.

WHERE THIS STORY CAME FROM

Myint Naing's story comes from interviews with him, his family, his friends and other former slaves, and through following his journey from a makeshift camp set up for rescued men at an Indonesian port in Tual, Indonesia, to his home in Myanmar. He's among hundreds rescued and returned to their families after a year-long AP investigation exposed extreme labor abuses in Southeast Asia's seafood industry. Reporters documented how slave-caught fish is shipped from Indonesia to Thailand. It can then be exported to the United States and cloud the supply chains of supermarkets and distributors, including Wal-Mart, Sysco and Kroger, and pet food brands, such as Fancy Feast, Meow Mix and Iams. The companies have all said they strongly condemn labor abuse and are taking steps to prevent it.

Chapter 4

SILVER SEA STORY

The Silver Sea Line, a 3,000-ton Thai cargo ship, is docked at the compound of a fishing company in Benjina, Indonesia. The ship belongs to the Silver Sea Reefer Co., which is registered in Thailand and has at least nine refrigerated cargo boats, November 22, 2014. (AP Photo/Dita Alangkara)

TRACKING WITH TECHNOLOGY
Yangon, Myanmar, Monday, July 27, 2015

From space, the fishing boats are just little white specks floating in a vast stretch of blue water off Papua New Guinea. But zoom in and there's the critical evidence: Two trawlers loading slave-caught seafood onto a massive refrigerated cargo ship.

The trawlers fled a slave island in Indonesia with captives of a brutal Southeast Asian trafficking ring whose catch reaches the United States. Hundreds of men were freed after they were discovered there earlier this year, but 34 boats loaded with workers left for new fishing grounds before help arrived - they remain missing.

After a four-month investigation, The Associated Press has found that at least some of them ended up in a narrow, dangerous strait nearly 1,000 miles away. The proof comes from accounts from recently returned slaves, satellite beacon tracking, government records, interviews with business insiders and fishing licenses. The location is also confirmed in images from space taken by one of the world's highest resolution satellite cameras, upon the AP's request.

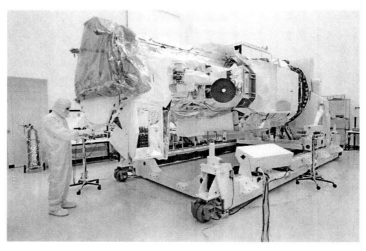

A technician runs tests on WorldView-3, a high-resolution imaging satellite operated by DigitalGlobe in Westminster, Colorado. The commercially owned company, supporting The Associated Press in its investigation into slavery in Southeast Asia's fishing industry, trained its satellite lenses on boats that are using forced laborers, May 13, 2014. (AP Photo/Brennan Linsley)

The skippers have changed their ships' names and flags to evade authorities, but hiding is easy in the world's broad oceans. Traffickers operate with impunity across boundaries as fluid as the waters. Laws are few and hardly enforced. And depleted fish stocks have pushed boats farther out into seas that are seldom even glimpsed, let alone governed.

This lack of regulation means that even with the men located, bringing them to safety may prove elusive.

Officials from Papua New Guinea working with the International Organization for Migration said they were not aware of human trafficking cases in the area but are investigating. Numerous other agencies - including Interpol, the United Nations and the U.S. State and Defense departments - told the AP they don't have the authority to get involved.

A handful of former slaves who recently made it home to Myanmar said hundreds of men remain unaccounted for.

"Papua New Guinea can be a lawless place," said Lin Lin, one of the returnees, describing fishing in the poor island nation. "Fishermen could die anytime, but the captains would not care. If they die, they will just be thrown away."

He said he and his crewmembers still don't know why they were sent home last month, when their trawler returned to the same port in Thailand from which they were originally trafficked.

As the appetite for cheap fish worldwide grows, so does the demand for men who are paid little or nothing to catch it. Thailand's $7 billion annual seafood export industry is built on the backs of poor people from its own country and migrants from Myanmar, Cambodia and Laos who are sold, kidnapped and tricked onto trawlers.

In November, the AP found hundreds of such forced laborers on the remote island village of Benjina in eastern Indonesia - some in a cage, others on boats and more than 60 buried in a graveyard. To date, the reporting has prompted the rescue and repatriation of more than 800 men, many of whom said they were abused or witnessed others being beaten, or in some cases even killed.

Reporters followed the slave-caught fish back to Thailand and linked it to the supply chains of major U.S. food sellers, such as Wal-Mart, Sysco and Kroger, and American pet food companies, including Fancy Feast, Meow Mix and Iams. The businesses have all said they strongly condemn labor abuse and vowed to take steps to prevent it.

In April, a week after the AP story was published, the Indonesian government launched a criminal inquiry. It was already clamping down on illegal fishing nationwide with a moratorium on all foreign boats. Officials rescued hundreds on the spot but they discovered that a third of the company's 90 trawlers had already left - each with 15 to 20 migrants on board. The Indonesian government wants to bring the boats back for prosecution.

"They have to be responsible for what's happened," said Fisheries Minister Susi Pudjiastuti.

The disappearing act can start with a bucket of paint.

Kaung Htet Wai, 25, said his crewmates nailed a new name and number over the old one - Antasena 331 - and hoisted a different country's flag: the red, black and yellow of Papua New Guinea. Wai said his trawler did not dock for several months, and loaded many types of seafood, including mackerel, shrimp and shark, onto refrigerated cargo ships. Captains also repainted and renumbered other boats, and some kept flags from as many as four different countries in their hulls, according to former slaves and investigators.

Former Burmese slave fisherman Kaung Htet Wai offers flowers at a Buddhist shrine in his house in Yangon, Myanmar. He recently returned from waters off Papua New Guinea, where he says dozens of boats fled a crackdown in neighboring Indonesia on illegal fishing. Recent returnees say hundreds of other men remain unaccounted for and are believed to be fishing by force in the same, dangerous waters, July 17, 2015. (AP Photo/Gemunu Amarasinghe)

The flag change protects rogue boats because typically the flagged states, not the host country, set their rules, said Mark Lagon, president of the Freedom House in Washington D.C. and former U.S. ambassador at large to combat human trafficking. Laws in general are weaker for fishing trawlers than other vessels, as is overall monitoring, he noted, creating a "black hole of governance."

As the boats hid, Indonesian investigators discovered that the company listed as their operator, Pusaka Benjina Resources, was really a venture between seafood industry tycoons and businessmen from Thailand and Indonesia.

Mark Lagon, President of Freedom House, speaks to an Associated Press reporter about slavery in the seafood industry at Freedom House in Washington, November 20, 2015. (AP Photo/Carolyn Kaster)

Financial records going back seven years reveal Pusaka Benjina's lucrative business with a shipping company, Silver Sea Fishery Co. The trawlers crewed by slaves brought fish to Benjina, where it was loaded onto Silver Sea cargo ships heading for Thailand.

In a typical month, Silver Sea was invoiced about $500,000 for loads of seafood. One month the firm was billed $1.6 million, with a third of that charged to the Silver Sea 2 - the same transport ship identified earlier this month in the satellite photo off Papua New Guinea.

Pusaka Benjina manager Hermanwir Martino, among seven people arrested on human trafficking charges, has said his company did nothing wrong. Silver Sea Fishery did not answer calls.

Photographs from the sky helped the AP actually catch the Silver Sea 2 in the act of doing business with the trawlers.

Over the past few months, satellite beacons show, Silver Sea cargo ships had been shuttling regularly between Thailand and Papua New Guinea. They slowed to a crawl or halted completely, apparently as they were being loaded with fish, in a crooked strait known as the dogleg.

Silver Sea 2, a Thai-owned cargo ship which was seized by Indonesian authorities in August, is docked at the port of Sabang, Aceh province, Indonesia. The Thai captain of the ship has been arrested in Indonesia following allegations of illegal fishing, September 25, 2015. (AP Photo/Heri Juanda)

Analysts at SkyTruth, a West Virginia remote sensing and digital mapping firm, identified the Silver Sea 2 by its signals. However, they warned that getting photographic evidence of it collecting fish from one of the trawlers that fled Benjina would be next to impossible.

Nonetheless, two weeks ago, DigitalGlobe, a Colorado-based commercial vendor of space imagery, maneuvered a satellite at the request of the AP toward coordinates of the Silver Sea 2, which had dropped anchor off Papua New Guinea. The cargo reefer struck experts as suspicious because it had turned off its locator beacon for almost two days, possibly while picking up seafood.

The satellite whizzed over Papua New Guinea at 17,000 mph, 380 miles up. Within a day, DigitalGlobe analysts spotted a high-resolution shot of a ship matching the Silver Sea 2 right down to the docking ropes and open cargo holds, with boats identical to those from Benjina nestled alongside, apparently offloading fish.

In this satellite image provided by DigitalGlobe, two fishing trawlers load slave-caught fish onto the Silver Sea 2, center, a refrigerated cargo ship belonging to the Thai-owned Silver Sea Fishery Co., off the coast of Papua New Guinea, July 14, 2015. (DigitalGlobe via AP)

CEO Jeff Tarr said this was the first time the technology had been used to capture human trafficking live: "You can't hide from space."

Gisa Komangin, from Papua New Guinea's National Fisheries Authority, said that until now their focus has been on illegal fishing in the dogleg, and that a moratorium on all foreign fishing there is planned for the end of the month to crack down on poaching.

"When you are talking about illegal fishing," he said, "you are also talking about human smuggling."

The question now is if the men will be rescued. Many governments lack the resources - or the will - to implement a patchwork of outdated maritime rules, some written more than a century ago. Kenneth Kennedy, a senior policy adviser for the U.S. Department of Homeland Security, said international fishing agreements on sustainability, pollution and labor are needed, and those that do exist often go unenforced.

"If all these corporations, or ships, are ignoring these things put in place for the future of humanity, then what are we doing?" he asked. "We're just spinning our wheels."

Back in a dusty slum in Myanmar, relatives of the slaves still missing are desperate. One mother, Ohn Myint, went to the airport three times as men rescued from Benjina came home - hoping her 19-year-old son, Myo Ko Ko, would come out of the terminal. But every time, she left alone, a little more drained of hope.

"I am missing my son so much, each and every hour," she said. "I can only pray for him. I just think that only God can save him."

Ohn Myint, mother of 19-year-old Myo Ko Ko, a Burmese slave believed to be trapped on a fishing trawler in a narrow strait off Papua New Guinea, weeps in Yangon, Myanmar. "I miss my son so much, each and every hour," she said. "All I can do is pray for him", July 16, 2015. (AP Photo/Gemunu Amarasinghe)

SEIZING THE SILVER SEA 2
Jakarta, Indonesia, Friday, August 14, 2015

A massive refrigerated cargo ship believed to be loaded with slave-caught fish was seized by Indonesia's navy and brought to shore Thursday, after The Associated Press informed authorities it had entered the country's waters.

The Thai-owned Silver Sea 2 was located late Wednesday and escorted about 80 miles (130 kilometers) to a naval base in Sabang on the Indonesian archipelago's northwestern tip, said Col. Sujatmiko, the local naval chief.

The AP used a satellite beacon signal to trace its path from Papua New Guinea waters, where it was also being sought, into neighboring Indonesia. The navy then spent a week trying to catch it. The ship was close to leaving Indonesian waters by the time it was finally seized.

"I'm so overwhelmed with happiness," said Fisheries Minister Susi Pudjiastuti, adding it was difficult to find because the boat's signal had a delay. "It was almost impossible, but we did it."

The Silver Sea 2 is the same 2,285-ton vessel captured in a high-resolution satellite photo last month in Papua New Guinea showing its hold open and two fishing trawlers tethered to each side, loading fish. Analysts identified the smaller trawlers as among those that fled the remote Indonesian island village of Benjina earlier this year, crewed by enslaved men from poor Southeast Asian countries who are routinely beaten and forced to work nearly nonstop with little or no pay.

DigitalGlobe imagery analyst Micah Farfour, shows a high-resolution satellite photograph taken of trawlers in Papua New Guinea loading slave-caught seafood onto Silver Sea 2, a refrigerated cargo ship belonging to the Thai-owned Silver Sea Fishery Co., at Digital-Globe's headquarters in Westminster, Colorado, July 17, 2015. (AP Photo/Brennan Linsley)

An AP investigation revealed their catch reached the supply chains of major U.S. food sellers, such as Wal-Mart, Sysco and Kroger, and American pet food companies, including Fancy Feast,

Meow Mix and Iams. The businesses have all said they strongly condemn labor abuse and vowed to take steps to prevent it.

Indonesia freed hundreds of men earlier this year after the AP exposed they were trapped - including some locked in a cage - on Benjina. But 34 boats loaded with slaves escaped before authorities arrived. They remain missing. Seven arrests have been made in Indonesia and two in Thailand related to the case.

Panya Luangsomboon, owner of Silver Sea Reefer Co., which owns several refrigerated cargo ships in Thailand, said Friday that the company has done nothing illegal and has asked Thai officials for help in getting the Silver Sea 2 back.

"We have received numerous calls from Thai agencies ... asking about this and basically we said we have never done anything like it," company manager Venus Pornpasert said Thursday of allegations of human trafficking and illegal fishing. Venus added that all of the ships' crews are Thai nationals and certified by the International Maritime Organization.

However, enslaved workers who recently returned home from Papua New Guinea to Myanmar said they had regularly loaded fish onto Silver Sea cargo ships, which ferried the catch back to Thailand. Burmese slaves rescued from Benjina, among hundreds interviewed by the AP in person or in writing, also said they had been trafficked in Thailand and brought to fish in Indonesia aboard the Silver Sea 2. And late last year, AP journalists saw slave-caught fish in Benjina being loaded onto another reefer owned by Silver Sea.

The Indonesian navy has so far declined to comment on the crew found aboard the captured vessel.

Pudjiastuti, who put a moratorium on all foreign boats last year to crack down on rampant poaching, said the Silver Sea 2 captain will be questioned, and an investigation will be launched into suspected human trafficking, transport of illegally caught fish and transshipment, which involves offloading fish at sea. It allows fishermen to work for months without returning to port, making it easier for their captains to exploit them.

Former fishing slaves who were rescued from Indonesia's remote island village of Benjina gather at a temporary government-run shelter on the island of Tual, Indonesia, April 20, 2015. (AP Photo/Margie Mason)

Crew of a Thai-owned cargo ship, Silver Sea 2, anchored off an Indonesian Navy base in Sabang, Aceh province, Indonesia, talk to a member of the Indonesian Navy, August 14, 2015. (AP Photo/Binsar Bakkara)

"Indonesia's action here is significant as it demonstrates a commitment to enforcing the actions of vessels within their waters, regardless of whether they are fishing illegally or trafficking labor," said Tobias Aguirre, executive director of California-based non-profit Fishwise, which advocates for sustainable, slave-free seafood.

Authorities in Papua New Guinea had also been searching for the boat. They instead seized another Thai-owned fish cargo ship, the Blissful Reefer, two weeks ago. Two trafficked Burmese and six Cambodians were found on board.

Indonesian police also are investigating trafficking claims involving 45 Burmese fishermen who were rescued from a Jakarta hotel last week. Arie Dharmanto, who heads the anti-human trafficking unit of the National Police, said the men had fake documents identifying themselves as Thai, and that officials from two Indonesian companies have been questioned about their role.

ARRESTING SLAVERS
Sabang, Indonesia, Saturday, September 26, 2015

The Thai captain of a seized cargo ship carrying an estimated $2 million worth of seafood has been arrested in Indonesia on suspicion of illegal fishing, in the latest development linked to an Associated Press investigation that uncovered a slave island earlier this year. At least one other crew member is still under scrutiny.

The massive Thai-owned Silver Sea 2 was first identified by AP in July through a high-resolution photo taken from space, showing slave-caught fish being loaded onto the refrigerated vessel in Papua New Guinea's waters. The AP then tracked the ship through its satellite beacon and informed Indonesian authorities when it crossed into their waters on its way home to Thailand.

Friday's arrest is one of at least 10 made in Indonesia and Thailand since the investigation tied the catch of migrant workers forced to fish to the supply chains of major U.S. food sellers and pet food companies six months ago. As a result, more than 2,000 men from Myanmar, Thailand, Cambodia and Laos have been identified or sent home, a multi-million dollar Thai-Indonesian fishing business has been shut down, class action lawsuits have been filed and new laws have been introduced.

Touring the Silver Sea 2 on Friday, Indonesian Fisheries Minister Susi Pudjiastuti said she believed the frozen fish filling up its holds came from eastern Indonesia's Arafura Sea, where foreign fishing vessels are banned. She also said authorities are looking further into evidence that suggests the ship may be linked to the human trafficking ring described by AP. The Silver Sea 2 is accused of receiving illegally caught fish at sea and turning off its satellite beacon. Its remaining 16 crew members will be deported.

Navy personnel stand guard as the crew of Silver Sea 2 are lined up during a media conference at the port of Sabang, September 25, 2015. (AP Photo/Heri Juanda)

Pudjiastuti said she hoped anyone found guilty would face harsh punishment as a deterrent, and added the vessel may be destroyed. Indonesia has already blown up dozens of smaller foreign boats accused of illegal fishing. The 2,285-ton ship is now at a naval base in Sabang in the country's far northwestern tip where it was seized last month.

"If the court decides it should be confiscated, then we will sink it," she said.

Silver Sea Reefer Co., which owns Silver Sea 2, maintains it has done nothing wrong.

Thailand's fishing industry, worth $7 billion a year in exports, relies on tens of thousands of poor migrant laborers who come seeking jobs mainly from neighboring countries. They often are tricked, sold or kidnapped and put onto boats sent to distant foreign waters to fish. Refrigerated cargo ships are used to pick up seafood and sometimes transport new slaves, although no victims of trafficking were found on the Silver Sea 2.

Indonesian Minister of Fisheries Susi Pudjiastuti, center, examines fish from the cargo bay of Silver Sea 2 at the port of Sabang, Aceh province, Indonesia, September 25, 2015. (AP Photo/Heri Juanda)

Late last year, AP journalists saw slave-caught fish being loaded onto another reefer owned by Silver Sea in the Indonesian island village of Benjina, where men were found locked in a cage for asking to go home. In written surveys conducted with nearly 400 rescued slaves, several also told AP they were trafficked to Indonesia from Thailand aboard Silver Sea ships, including Silver Sea 2.

The high-resolution photo taken from space for AP by U.S.-based commercial satellite imagery company DigitalGlobe showed the Silver Sea 2 in Papua New Guinea with its holds open and a trawler tethered to each side, loading fish. Analysts identified the smaller boats as among those that fled Benjina earlier this year, crewed by enslaved men who said they were routinely beaten and forced to work nearly nonstop with little or no pay. Another Thai cargo ship was also impounded in Papua New Guinea after eight trafficking victims were found on board.

Indonesian Minister of Fisheries Susi Pudjiastuti shows a photograph taken from a surveillance plane in July showing two trawlers loading seafood onto Silver Sea 2, a Thai-owned cargo ship which was seized by Indonesian authorities last August, at the port of Sabang, Aceh province, Indonesia, September 25, 2015. (AP Photo/Heri Juanda)

The AP's work was entered into the U.S. congressional record for a hearing, after links were made to the supply chains of American companies such as Wal-Mart, Sysco, Kroger, Fancy Feast, Meow Mix and Iams. The businesses have all said they strongly condemn labor abuse and have taken steps to prevent it. Congress is scheduled to discuss the AP findings again later this month.

Chapter 5

IN SPITE OF THE LAW

An Indonesian official inspects a cell at the compound of Pusaka Benjina Resources fishing company in Benjina, Aru Islands, Indonesia, April 2, 2015. (AP Photo/Dita Alangkara)

INDUCED ACTION
Benjina, Indonesia, Friday, April 3, 2015

Officials from three countries are traveling to remote islands in eastern Indonesia to investigate how thousands of foreign fishermen were abused and forced into catching seafood that could end up in the United States, Europe and elsewhere.

A week after The Associated Press published a story about slavery in the seafood industry - including video of men locked in a cage - delegations from Thailand and Indonesia visited the island village of Benjina. A government team from Myanmar, otherwise known as Burma, is also scheduled to tour the area next week to try to determine how many of its citizens are stuck there and what can be done to bring them home.

A Thai official inspects a cell at the compound of Pusaka Benjina Resources fishing company in Benjina, Aru Islands, Indonesia, April 1, 2015. (AP Photo/Dita Alangkara)

The visits reflect how the problem stretches across several countries, and how difficult it has been to resolve. The migrant workers lured or even kidnapped into fishing are usually from Myanmar, one of the poorest countries in the world, along with Cambodia, Laos and impoverished areas of Thailand. They are brought from Thailand to fishing boats in Indonesia, where many say they are beaten, made to work long hours with little or no pay, and prevented from leaving. Their catch is then shipped back to Thailand, where it enters global markets, the AP story documented.

On Thursday, the atmosphere was tense as a group of Burmese men in Benjina talked nervously to the AP. One older fisherman with dark, weathered skin recounted how he was recruited from Myanmar and promised a good job in neighboring Thailand, but was sent to Indonesia instead. He said he had been working for six and a half years on boats in Indonesia, where the captain would swear at him and kick him in the ribs with boots.

"I know talking to you is dangerous, that our lives are threatened, but this is the only way to get out of here," he said. The AP is withholding the men's names out of safety concerns. "I just want to go home to see my parents before they die."

About a dozen fishing boats were docked on shore, while others bobbed far out enough in the water that officials could not see the crews. When the AP tried to interview Burmese workers on one boat, security guards at Pusaka Benjina Resources, the company that runs the fishing operation, barked into their radios and ran to stop the men from talking. Site manager Herman Martino said men were not allowed to speak to the press while on the trawlers.

Martino said there are about 1,000 fishermen in Benjina. At first, he said all were Thai. However, when pressed, he acknowledged that their official documents identified them as Thai, but it's possible some were from Myanmar, Cambodia, Laos and Vietnam.

Martino also denied allegations of slavery and said that although hours are irregular, workers are given time to rest and do not labor up to 22 hours a day, as many fishermen have reported. He tried to explain the cage the AP earlier found inside the company compound with eight men locked inside.

"What is described as a detention house is merely a temporary place, which is endorsed by immigration, to accommodate those committing light crimes such as theft, drunkenness or fighting among themselves on board," he said. "They were handed over by their Thai captains."

Immigration officials have denied any knowledge of the cell.

Benjina was one of several island stops this week for the government officials, who talked with migrant workers and visited a graveyard where dozens of fishermen were buried. Thai officials said they had already located and repatriated some Thai workers. However, they denied any mistreatment on the boats and said the crews were all Thai. Many of the men seen by the AP aboard trawlers and on the island were Burmese.

"We examined the boats and the crews, and the result is most of the crews are happy and a few of them are sick and willing to go home," said Thai police Lt. Gen. Saritchai Anekwiang, who was leading the delegation. "Generally, the boat conditions are good."

While Benjina was the site of some of the worst abuses, up to 4,000 men - many trafficked or enslaved - are now abandoned and stranded across surrounding islands, according to the International Organization for Migration. An Indonesian official from the Fisheries Ministry, Ida Kusuma, said she found the slavery reports very upsetting and promised action.

"We (will) prove that we don't want to let it happen anymore," she said, on the neighboring island of Tual.

Foreign fishermen sit on the ground before being questioned by Indonesian officials at the compound of Pusaka Benjina Resources fishing company in Benjina, April 3, 2015. (AP Photo/Dita Alangkara)

At the port in the provincial capital of Ambon, more than 800 kilometers (500 miles) from Benjina, runaways from Cambodia and Laos also described years of abuse. The AP visited a Christian cemetery where more than 20 white markers simply read "Thailand" in black print. It is unclear, however, whether the men were actually Thai nationals, since the AP found that many migrant workers from elsewhere are given fake documents with Thai names and addresses.

"If I was American, I know I would not eat fish," said one Cambodian who was trafficked at age 13 to Thailand and on to Indonesia. He's now 27 and has spent half of his life away from home. "It's so bad."

Just as worker documents are faked, so are fishing licenses, according to the Indonesian government. The fishing grounds in the Arafura Sea near Benjina are so rich that they attract illegal boats from Thailand and other countries, making it difficult to monitor labor practices.

Susi Pudjiastuti, Indonesia's new fisheries minister, has called a moratorium on fishing so that officials can review licenses. She has confiscated and blown up several illegal boats on television to send the message that Indonesian waters can no longer be plundered.

The ministry believes many of the ships fly Indonesian flags when in the country's waters, and then switch to another country's flag when leaving. In Tual on Tuesday, Kusuma said she was surprised to find a Chinese flag in the captain's room on one ship. The boat's Chinese name could also still be seen written in characters beneath a thin layer of white paint, and the captain was Chinese, she said.

"It's an Indonesian boat because it is registered in Indonesia and we also give license to them to fish," she said. "They shouldn't have to fly both flags, whatever the reason is."

The AP investigation used satellites to track seafood caught by the slaves from Benjina to Thailand, and documented links to the supply chains of some of America's largest supermarkets and retailers. The report prompted the U.S. government and major seafood industry leaders to urge Thailand to end slavery at sea and to punish those responsible. The State Department is monitoring the situation closely, an official said in an emailed statement.

In the meantime, the graffiti scratched on the walls of the cell - poems, names of loved ones, simple sketches of monks - is a testimony to the despair and longing of the men who have been housed there.

"I hope I will get home in time," one poem says. "If there is a way in, there is a way out."

"It's so painful to be a seaman," another reads. "I have no attachment anymore."

14 YEARS AND THEY ARE STILL DOING IT
Washington, Wednesday, April 22, 2015

In its first report on trafficking around the world, the U.S. criticized Thailand as a hub for labor abuse. Yet 14 years later, seafood caught by slaves on Thai boats is still slipping into the supply chains of major American stores and supermarkets.

The U.S. has not enforced a law banning the import of goods made with forced labor since 2000 because of significant loopholes,

The Associated Press has found. It has also spared Thailand from sanctions slapped on other countries with weak records in human trafficking because of a complex political relationship that includes cooperation against terrorism.

Matthew Smith, executive director of the Thailand-based Fortify Rights, testifies before the House Committee on Foreign Affairs subcommittee on Africa, Global Health, Global Human Rights, and International Organizations hearing on the fight against human trafficking, in Washington, April 22, 2015. (AP Photo/Cliff Owen)

The question of how to deal with Thailand and labor abuse will come up at a congressional hearing Wednesday, in light of an AP investigation that found hundreds of men beaten, starved, forced to work with little or no pay and even held in a cage on the remote island village of Benjina. While officials at federal agencies would not directly answer why the law and sanctions are not applied, they pointed out that the U.S. State Department last year blacklisted Thailand as among the worst offenders in its report on trafficking in people worldwide.

Phil Robertson, deputy director of Human Rights Watch's Asia division, said the plight of about 4,000 forced laborers in Thailand's seafood industry can no longer go unheeded. Many are migrant workers from Myanmar and other countries who were forced to work on Thai boats in Indonesian waters.

"There have been problems with systematic and pervasive human trafficking in Thailand's fishing fleets for more than a decade, but Washington has evidently considered it too hard to find out exactly what was happening and is not taking action to stop it," he said. "No one can claim ignorance anymore. This is a test case for Washington as much as Bangkok."

Hlaing Min, a 32-year-old migrant fisherman from Myanmar who worked around the clock for more than two years before he ran away, also begged the U.S. for help.

"Basically, we are slaves - and slavery is the only word that I can find - but our condition is worse than slavery," he said. "On behalf of all the fishermen here, I request to the congressmen that the U.S. stop buying all fish from Thailand. ... This fish, we caught it with our blood and sweat, but we don't get a single benefit from it."

The AP investigation tracked fish caught by slaves to the supply chains of large food sellers such as Wal-Mart, Sysco and Kroger, as well as popular brands of canned pet food such as Fancy Feast, Meow Mix and Iams. The companies all said they strongly condemn labor abuse and are taking steps to prevent it. While some human rights advocates say boycotts are effective, many U.S. seafood companies say cutting off all imports from an entire country means they no longer have any power to bring about change.

During a recent visit to Jakarta, State Department Undersecretary Catherine A. Novelli was asked what the U.S. would now do.

"I'm sure that your public would be concerned that the fish that they ate came from a slave," said an Indonesian reporter.

Novelli's response was quick.

"In the United States we actually have a law that it is illegal to import any product that is made with forced labor or slave labor, and that includes fish," she said. "To the extent that we can trace ... where the fish are coming from, we won't allow fish to come into the United States that has been produced with forced labor or slavery."

However, the Tariff Act of 1930, which gives Customs and Border Protection the authority to seize shipments where forced labor is suspected and block further imports, has been used only 39 times in 85 years. In 11 cases, the orders detaining shipments were later revoked.

Catherine A. Novelli testifies during a hearing of the Subcommittee on Consumer Protection, Product Safety, and Insurance in Washington, May 19 2011. (AP Photo/Alex Brandon)

The most recent case dates back to 2000, when Customs stopped clothing from Mongolian firm Dong Fang Guo Ji based on evidence that factory managers forced employees, including children, to work 14-hour days for low wages. The order was revoked in 2001, after further review found labor abuse was no longer a problem at the company.

Detention orders that remain in place can have mixed results.

In 1999, Customs blocked hand-rolled unfiltered cigarettes from the Mangalore Ganesh Beedie Works in India, suspecting child labor. However, the AP found that Mangalore Ganesh has sent 11 large shipments of the cigarettes to Beedies LLC of Kissimee, Florida, over the past four years through the ports of New York, Miami and Savannah, Georgia. Beedies LLC said the cigarettes go straight from the U.S. ports to a bonded warehouse, and are then exported outside the country.

To start an investigation, Customs needs to receive a petition from anyone - a business, an agency, even a non-citizen - showing "reasonably but not conclusively" that imports were made at least in part with forced labor. But spokesman Michael Friel said that in the last four years, Customs has received "only a handful of petitions," and none has pointed to seafood from Thailand. The most recent petition was filed two years ago by a non-profit against cotton in Uzbekistan.

"These cases often involve numerous allegations that require extensive agency investigation and fact-finding," he said.

Experts also point to two gaping loopholes in the law. Goods made with forced labor must be allowed into the U.S. if consumer demand cannot be met without them. And it's hard, if not impossible, to prove fish in a particular container is tainted, because different batches generally mix together at processing plants.

Former Justice Department attorney Jim Rubin said Customs can't stop trafficked goods without the help of other federal agencies to investigate overseas.

"You can't expect a Customs guy at the border to know that a can of salmon caught on the high seas was brought in by a slave," he said.

The U.S. response to Thailand is also shaped by political considerations.

For years, the State Department has put Thailand on the watchlist in its annual trafficking report, saying the Thai government has made efforts to stop labor abuse. But last year, after several waivers, it dropped Thailand for the first time to the lowest rank, mentioning forced labor in the seafood industry. Countries with the same ranking, such as Cuba, Iran and North Korea, faced full sanctions, and foreign aid was withheld. Others, like Sudan, Syria and Zimbabwe, faced partial sanctions.

Thailand did not: U.S. taxpayers provided $18.5 million in foreign aid to the country last year.

"If Thailand was North Korea or Iran, they'd be treated differently," said Josh Kurlantzick, a fellow for Southeast Asia at the Council on Foreign Relations. "They're a key ally and we have a long relationship with them."

In the 1960s and '70s, when the U.S. needed Thailand's help in the Vietnam War, the country "got a pass on everything," Kurlantzick said. Then Thailand's record on human rights gradually improved, along with its economy. That changed dramatically in 2006, when the military first ousted the prime minister. It declared martial law and then overtook the government again last year.

In response, the U.S. condemned the current regime and has suspended $4.7 million in military funding to the Southeast Asian nation.

Secretary of State Colin Powell holds up the State Department's third annual report on human trafficking during a news conference in Washington, June 11, 2003. (AP Photo/Charles Dharapak)

However, the U.S. still includes Thailand in military exercises, and the country is considered a critical ally against terrorism. A U.S. Senate report in December detailed how top al-Qaida suspect Abu Zubaydah was waterboarded, slammed into a wall and isolated at a secret safe house in Thailand as part of CIA interrogations in 2002. And in 2003, a senior al-Qaida operative was arrested outside Bangkok after more than 200 people died in a Bali nightclub bombing.

The U.S. also wants strong relations with Thailand as a counterweight to China, whose influence is growing in the region.

Along with the State Department, the Labor Department has also flagged seafood from Thailand year after year as produced by forced labor in violation of international standards. Department of Homeland Security senior policy adviser Kenneth Kennedy referred to discussions for an action plan on labor abuse in Thailand that began in the fall.

"I think the U.S. government recently has realized that we need to pay attention to this area," he said. "We need to address conditions that have been reported for years and that are in the public minds and in the public eye very much."

Thailand itself says it is tackling labor abuse. In 2003, the country launched a national campaign against criminal organizations, including traffickers. In 2008, it adopted a new anti-human trafficking law. And last month, the new junta government cited the fight against trafficking as a national priority.

"This government is determined and committed to solving the human trafficking issues, not by words but by actions," deputy government spokesman Maj. Gen. Sansern Kaewkamnerd said. "We are serious in prosecuting every individual involved in the network, from the boats' captains to government officials."

However, a Thai police general on a fact-finding mission earlier this month to Benjina declared conditions were good and workers "happy." A day later, Indonesian authorities rescued more than 320 abused fishermen from the island village, and the number of workers waiting to be sent home has since risen to more than 560.

Under United Nations principles adopted in 2011, governments must protect against human rights abuses by third parties. However, some local authorities in Thailand are themselves deeply implicated in such practices, said Harvard University professor John Ruggie, who wrote the principles, known as the "Ruggie Framework," as a U.N. special representative. Also, Thailand's seafood industry, with annual exports of about $7 billion, is big business for the country and depends on migrant labor.

Migrant fishermen rescued from Benjina were bewildered to learn that their abuse has been an open secret for years. Maung Htwe, a 26-year-old migrant worker from Myanmar, did backbreaking work for Thai captains in Indonesian waters over seven years, earning less than $5 a day, if he was lucky.

"Sometimes I'm really angry. It's so painful. Why was I sold and taken to Indonesia?" asked Htwe, who was among the workers rescued from Benjina. "If people already knew the story, then they should have helped us and taken action."

INDONESIAN POLICE ARREST SEVEN
Jakarta, Indonesia, Wednesday, May 13, 2015

Two Indonesians and five Thais were arrested on charges of human trafficking connected with slavery in the seafood industry, Indonesian police said. They were the first suspects taken into custody since the case was revealed by The Associated Press in a report two months ago.

The arrests were made Monday and late Friday in the remote island village of Benjina, said Lt. Col. Arie Dharmanto, National Police anti-trafficking unit chief.

Five Thai boat captains and two Indonesian employees at Pusaka Benjina Resources, one of the largest fishing firms in eastern Indonesia, were taken into custody. The arrests come after the AP reported on slave-caught seafood shipped from Benjina to Thailand, where it can be exported and enter the supply chains of some of America's biggest food retailers.

"They have committed an extraordinary crime, and we will not let it happen again in Indonesia," Dharmanto said Tuesday. "We will not stop here. We will pursue those who are involved in this case, whoever they are."

Police will recommend they be charged by prosecutors. If the men go to trial, they could face jail sentences of up to 15 years and fines as high as $46,000, he said.

He said the number of suspects would likely climb because authorities are still investigating how thousands of foreign fishermen from Myanmar, Cambodia, Laos and Thailand were put on fishing boats in Thailand - sometimes after being tricked or kidnapped - and brought to work in Indonesian waters where they were not allowed to leave. Many said they were beaten and forced to work up to 24 hours a day with inadequate food and unclean water. Most were paid little or nothing at all.

The yearlong AP investigation found that tainted fish can wind up in the supply chains of some of America's biggest food sellers, such as Wal-Mart, Sysco and Kroger. It can also find its way into the supply chains of some of the most popular brands of canned pet food, including Fancy Feast, Meow Mix and Iams. The companies have all said they strongly condemn labor abuse and are taking steps to prevent it, such as working with human rights groups to hold subcontractors accountable.

An Indonesian official puts wrist bands on recently rescued Burmese fishermen for identification purpose upon their arrival in Tual, Indonesia. Two Indonesians and five Thais were arrested on charges of human trafficking connected with slavery in the seafood industry, said Indonesian police Lt. Col. Arie Dharmanto, National Police anti-trafficking unit chief, April 4, 2015. (AP Photo/Dita Alangkara)

Gavin Gibbons, spokesman for the National Fisheries Institute, which represents about 75 percent of U.S. seafood sellers, said they are eager to see the cases prosecuted.

"This is exactly the kind of action we've called for," he said Tuesday. "We are pleased to see the government of Indonesia working swiftly to investigate and acting to arrest suspects in this incident."

In April, a week after the story was published, Indonesia's Fisheries Ministry made a dramatic rescue when officials loaded more than 300 slaves and former slaves in Benjina onto six fishing boats for a 17-hour overnight voyage to the island of Tual where they have since been housed at a makeshift camp near the port.

With 59 Cambodians returning home Monday, most of those remaining are from Myanmar, otherwise known as Burma, but a few are also from Laos. More than 200 others have also been identified in Benjina and are waiting for travel documents to go home as well.

Dharmanto said authorities planned to fly all the suspects to Indonesia's capital, Jakarta, after the investigation is completed.

Police were still questioning the company's security guards, who were also expected to be named as suspects, he added.

He said the police probe found that hundreds of foreign fishermen were recruited in Thailand and brought to Indonesia using fake immigration papers and seamen books and were subjected to brutal labor abuses. The suspects are accused of locking fishermen up for one to six months in a prison-like cell located in the company's compound in Benjina.

Police have seized five fishing boats allegedly used by the suspects for human trafficking and slavery-like practices as well as dozens of fake passports and seamen books.

Dharmanto said the arrests were made after police questioned more than 50 foreign fishermen from Myanmar and Cambodia along with 16 witnesses, including company employees, immigration and port officials.

TRAFFICKING BROKERS ARRESTED
Bangkok, Thailand, Wednesday, July 1, 2015

Two Thai men described as key figures in a human trafficking ring that provides slave crews for fishing boats were arrested, officials said Wednesday, as new regulations aimed at cracking down on illegal fishing took effect.

The two suspects were the latest to be arrested following an Associated Press investigation into slavery in Southeast Asia's fishing industry.

In April, the EU gave Thailand six months to drastically combat illegal and unregulated fishing or face a seafood import ban. Thailand is a major exporter of seafood, with yearly revenues of almost 5 billion euros ($5.4 billion), and an EU ban would seriously affect the industry.

Officials from Thailand's Department of Special Investigation told a news conference the two men were "big figures" in a human trafficking syndicate in Samut Sakorn province, the country's biggest fishing hub, and had lured about 60 victims a year since 2008.

Chayuthphong Charoenporn, 50, and Samruay Chatkrod, 53, hired middlemen to find workers at train stations, bus terminals and other public places, said Lt. Col. Komvich Padhanarath.

An investigator of Thailand's Department of Special Investigation interrogates a key suspect in a human trafficking ring Samruay Chatkrod, left, in Bangkok, Thailand, July 1, 2015. (AP Photo/Sakchai Lalit)

Komvich said the middlemen would approach men who looked poor and ask them if they wanted jobs and then take them to a shelter where they were sometimes drugged or given alcohol to keep quiet - and then sold to boat owners for 30,000 baht ($900) per person. The laborers were then taken without their consent to fishing boats near Ambon island in Indonesia, he said.

"These two illegal brokers are quite big figures," said Paisith Sungkahapong, director of the human trafficking division at the DSI, which is Thailand's equivalent of the FBI. He said they admitted to human trafficking, which carries a maximum penalty of life in prison or capital punishment, but denied the charges of arbitrary detention.

"They were trying to persuade people and deceive those people to work in the fishing boats," Paisith said, adding that many of the laborers didn't know they were agreeing to work on boats let alone in a foreign country. "They did not know they would be working overseas."

Also Wednesday, the Thai government's new Fisheries Act took effect. The law was drafted to improve official oversight and impose stricter measures to prevent illegal practices in the Thai fishing industry, which has come under mounting pressure from the EU.

Under the new regulations, all fishing boats are required to hold licenses, registration and legal fishing equipment and navigation systems that can be traced by authorities.

The new rules have met with resistance from fishermen who demanded that the deadline of July 1 be extended. At least 1,000 fishing trawlers in the southern province of Songkhla threatened to go on strike from Friday and asked the government to help them through the transition.

"They are now in deep trouble because if they go out, they are afraid they will be arrested. Then they will have to pay a fine of more than 100,000 baht ($30,000) or go to jail. It's too much," said Praporn Ekouru, the Songkhla Fishery Association's chairman.

Prime Minister Prayuth Chan-ocha on Wednesday asked for cooperation from the fishing companies to comply with the new rules.

"If we don't pass (the EU) evaluation, will they share the responsibility of losing the products worth more than 2 billion baht that we can't sell to the entire world?" he asked, pleading with them not to strike.

SEAFOOD SUPPLIER LABOR ABUSE ADMITTED
Washington, Monday, November 23, 2015

Impoverished migrant workers in Thailand are sold or lured by false promises and forced to catch and process fish that ends up in global food giant Nestle SA's supply chains.

The unusual disclosure comes from Geneva-based Nestle SA itself, which in an act of self-policing announced the conclusions of its yearlong internal investigation on Monday. The study found virtually all U.S. and European companies buying seafood from Thailand are exposed to the same risks of abuse in their supply chains.

Nestle SA, among the biggest food companies in the world, launched the investigation in December 2014, after reports from news outlets and nongovernmental organizations tied brutal and largely unregulated working conditions to their shrimp, prawns and Purina brand pet foods. Its findings echo those of The Associated Press in reports this year on slavery in the seafood industry that have resulted in the rescue of more than 2,000 fishermen.

Workers in Benjina, Indonesia, load fish into a cargo ship bound for Thailand, November 22, 2014. (AP Photo/Dita Alangkara)

The laborers come from Thailand's much poorer neighbors Myanmar and Cambodia. Brokers illegally charge them fees to get jobs, trapping them into working on fishing vessels and at ports, mills and seafood farms in Thailand to pay back more money than they can ever earn.

"Sometimes, the net is too heavy and workers get pulled into the water and just disappear. When someone dies, he gets thrown into the water," one Burmese worker told the nonprofit organization Verite commissioned by Nestle.

"I have been working on this boat for 10 years. I have no savings. I am barely surviving," said another. "Life is very difficult here."

Nestle said it would post the reports online - as well as a detailed yearlong solution strategy throughout 2016 - as part of ongoing efforts to protect workers. It has promised to impose new requirements on all potential suppliers and train boat owners and captains about human rights, possibly with a demonstration vessel and rewards for altering their practices. It also plans to bring in outside auditors and assign a high-level Nestle manager to make sure change is underway.

"As we've said consistently, forced labor and human rights abuses have no place in our supply chain," Magdi Batato, Nestle's executive vice president in charge of operations, said in a written statement. "Nestle believes that by working with suppliers we can make a positive difference to the sourcing of ingredients."

Nestle is not a major purchaser of seafood in Southeast Asia but does some business in Thailand, primarily for its Purina brand Fancy Feast cat food.

For its study, Verite interviewed more than 100 people, including about 80 workers from Myanmar and Cambodia, as well as boat owners, shrimp farm owners, site supervisors and representatives of Nestle's suppliers. They visited fish ports and fishmeal packing plants, shrimp farms and docked fishing boats, all in Thailand.

A shrimp farmer leaves a platform after feeding shrimp in a pond in Mahachai, Thailand. When farmers in Asia started growing shrimp in ponds three decades ago, Thailand quickly dominated the market, October 1, 2015. (AP Photo/Gemunu Amarasinghe)

Boat captains and managers, along with workers, confirmed violence and danger in the Thai seafood sector, a booming industry which exports $7 billion of products a year, although managers said workers sometimes got hurt because they were drunk and fighting. Boat captains rarely checked ages of workers, and Verite found underage workers forced to fish. Workers said they labor without rest, their food and water are minimal, outside contact is cut off, and they are given fake identities to hide that they are working illegally.

Generally, the workers studied by Verite were catching and processing fish into fishmeal fed to shrimp and prawns. But the Amherst, Massachusetts-based group said many of the problems they observed are systemic and not unique to Nestle; migrant workers throughout Thailand's seafood sector are vulnerable to abuses as they are recruited, hired and employed, said Verite.

Monday's disclosure is rare. While multinational companies in industries from garments to electronics say they investigate allegations of abuse in their supply chains, they rarely share negative findings.

"It's unusual and exemplary," said Mark Lagon, president of the nonprofit Freedom House, a Washington-based anti-trafficking organization. "The propensity of the PR and legal departments of companies is not to 'fess up, not to even say they are carefully looking into a problem for fear that they will get hit with lawsuits," he said.

In fact, Nestle is already being sued: In August, pet food buyers filed a class-action lawsuit alleging Fancy Feast cat food was the product of slave labor associated with Thai Union Frozen Products, a major distributor. It's one of several lawsuits filed in recent months against major U.S. retailers importing seafood from Thailand.

Some of the litigation cites the reports from the AP, which tracked slave-caught fish to the supply chains of giant food sellers, such as Wal-Mart, Sysco and Kroger, and popular brands of canned pet food, such as Fancy Feast, Meow Mix and Iams. It can turn up as calamari at fine restaurants, as imitation crab in a sushi roll or as packages of frozen snapper relabeled with store brands that land on dinner tables. The U.S. companies have all said they strongly condemn labor abuse and are taking steps to prevent it.

Nestle promises to publicly report its progress each year.

Chapter 6

OVER 2000 RESCUED
AND COUNTING

Former fishing slaves gather at their temporary shelter in Tual, Indonesia. Hundreds of former slaves rescued by the Indonesian government from the remote island of Benjina following the Associated Press investigation into slavery in seafood industry are now waiting to be repatriated, April 20, 2015. (AP Photo/Margie Mason)

STRANDED FISHERMEN
Jakarta, Indonesia, Wednesday, March 28, 2015

The number of foreign fishermen stranded on several remote eastern Indonesian islands has spiraled to 4,000, including some revealed in an Associated Press investigation to have been enslaved.

Many are migrant workers abandoned by their boat captains after the government passed a moratorium on foreign fishing five months ago, according to the International Organization for Migration, which released the figure Friday. However, others have been trapped on the islands for years, after being dumped by fishing boats or escaping into the jungle.

"This is the worst moment in our life right now," one former slave told the AP, which is not releasing the names of the men for their safety. "It is even worse than being in hell. We have to work every day to survive. ... There is no hope for us anymore."

The AP reported earlier this week that slaves - some of them beaten and locked in cages - are forced to fish, and their catch ends up in the supply chains of American supermarkets and restaurants. The migration agency said Friday that the report follows several years of close work with Indonesian authorities to rescue hundreds of fisherman identified as victims of trafficking.

Many of the stranded are men from Myanmar who went to neighboring Thailand in search of work. They were taken by boat to Indonesia, which has some of the world's richest fishing grounds. Others left behind on the islands are Cambodian and a few from the poorer parts of Thailand.

Steve Hamilton, IOM's deputy chief of mission in Indonesia, said for every man they've already rescued, many more now need help. With the fishing ban, boats have docked or fled, ditching their crews.

"It is reasonable to expect many are victims of trafficking, if not outright slavery," he said.

"But for the first time in possibly several years, their feet are touching dry land and there is a real possibility for them to go home, once we and the authorities locate and process them," he said.

About a quarter of the men are in Benjina, a town that straddles two islands in the Maluku chain, according to an Indonesian official who recently visited the area. These men, some abandoned five, 10, even 20 years ago, load and unload fish off boats for food and pocket money, or cut and sell logs in the forest of surrounding areas.

When the AP showed up, asking the men to share their stories, only a few emerged at first out of fear. Then, more and more filtered in, until a group of around 30 formed. Most squatted or sat on the ground, others stood around them as they recounted the horrors they had witnessed at sea. Then one after another, they expressed their desperate desire to go home, saying they were sure their families thought they were dead.

"Our body is here but our mind is at home," one dockworker said. "If it was possible to walk back home, we would do it right away."

Workers unload frozen fish from a Thai fishing boat at a port in Ambon, Indonesia, April 3, 2014. (AP Photo/Dita Alangkara)

Another wiped tears as he spoke, his voice quivering.

"Our lives have no more value than a dog," he said, adding no one cared if they lived or died. The AP is not using the men's names for their safety.

The moratorium was declared by Indonesia's new Fisheries Minister Susi Pudjiastuti to determine which ships are not properly licensed and crack down on illegal foreign boats. Poaching drains billions of dollars from the country, and Pudjiastuti said Friday that stamping it out is key to addressing labor abuses. She added she was horrified knowing fishermen are being enslaved in her country.

"We are not letting this happen," she said. "In the past, it's been a normal practice. Not now. I'm not allowing it."

The Indonesian government has pledged to take legal measures to address what is happening in Benjina and other islands. Thai Prime Minister Prayuth Chan-ocha also acknowledged the AP story and said his government was stepping up efforts to prosecute those responsible.

Thailand's Prime Minister Prayuth Chan-Ocha addresses world leaders at the COP21, United Nations Climate Change Conference, in Le Bourget, outside Paris, November 30, 2015. (AP Photo/Michel Euler)

"If they still continue to exploit their fellow human beings, they should not be given any licenses to operate businesses in Thailand, and they must receive the punishment they deserve," Prayuth said in a written response to questions submitted by the Bangkok Post.

However, earlier this week, Prayuth urged journalists not to report on human trafficking without considering how the news would affect the country's seafood industry and reputation abroad.

The U.S. State Department last year blacklisted Thailand for its handling of labor abuses, putting it on par with countries including North Korea and Iran. The Thai government says it is cleaning up the problem and has laid out a plan, including new laws that mandate wages, sick leave and shifts of no more than 14 hours. On Thursday, Thai lawmakers voted unanimously to create tougher penalties for violating the country's anti-human trafficking law, including the death penalty.

On Friday, 21 Thai fishermen who had been stranded in Indonesia returned home to their families, and the government is working to repatriate more.

Major leaders in the U.S. seafood and retail industries sent a letter to the ambassadors of Thailand and Indonesia this week, demanding to know what will be done to free slaves in the seafood industry. Phil Robertson, deputy director of Human Rights Watch's Asia division, also urged Thai authorities to tackle the scourge.

"The Thailand government has made repeated verbal commitments to get tough with traffickers but every time real follow-up has been lacking," Robertson said in an email. "The question now is whether the revelations in AP's article will finally be enough to push Thailand to take long overdue action against fishing vessels that are systematically using slave labor to catch the seafood ending up in America's kitchens."

Phil Robertson, deputy director of Human Rights Watch's Asia division, March 12, 2015 (AP Photo/Heng Sinith)

In the meantime, Ngwe Thein, 42, is one of the thousands of men who are waiting. Thein has been living on an island near Benjina for three years, after being forced to work long hours on a fishing trawler with inadequate food and little or no pay.

He said he left Myanmar, otherwise known as Burma, eight years ago when his country was still under military rule. He did not know about the political and economic changes that began sweeping his country in 2011 or that the oppressive and brutal junta was gone. He asked if Nobel prize-winning opposition leader Aung San Suu Kyi was still under house arrest.

Hours after the AP talked to him, he got a haircut and changed into a crisp shirt, saying he had hope for the first time that he might get to go home.

"I don't know whether our country is good or bad now," he said. "There is just always a problem for us to survive wherever we are."

AP INVESTIGATION PROMPTS EMERGENCY RESCUE
Benjina, Indonesia, Friday, April 3, 2015

At first the men filtered in by twos and threes, hearing whispers of a possible rescue.

Then, as the news rippled around the island, hundreds of weathered former and current slaves with long, greasy hair and tattoos streamed from their trawlers, down the hills, even out of the jungle, running toward what they had only dreamed of for years: Freedom.

Rescued Burmese fishermen raise their hands as they are asked who among them wants to go home at the compound of Pusaka Benjina Resources fishing company in Benjina, April 3, 2015. (AP Photo/Dita Alangkara)

"I will go see my parents. They haven't heard from me, and I haven't heard from them since I left," said Win Win Ko, 42, beaming, his smile showing missing teeth. The captain on his fishing boat had kicked out four teeth with his military boots, he said, because Win was not moving fish fast enough from the deck to the hold below.

The Burmese men were among hundreds of migrant workers revealed in an Associated Press investigation to have been lured or tricked into leaving their countries and forced into catching fish for consumers around the world, including the United States. In response to the AP's findings, Indonesian government officials visited the island village of Benjina on Friday and found brutal conditions, down to an "enforcer" paid to beat men up. They offered immediate evacuation.

The officials first gave the invitation for protection just to a small group of men who talked openly about their abuse. But then Asep Burhanuddin, director general of Indonesia's Marine Resources and Fisheries Surveillance, said everybody was welcome, including those hiding in the forest because they were too scared to go out.

"They can all come," he said. "We don't want to leave a single person behind."

Burmese fishermen wait to depart the compound of Pusaka Benjina Resources fishing company, April 3, 2015. (AP Photo/Dita Alangkara)

About 320 men took up the offer. Even as a downpour started, some dashed through the rain. They sprinted back to their boats, jumped over the rails and threw themselves through windows. They stuffed their meager belongings into plastic bags, small suitcases and day packs, and rushed back to the dock, not wanting to be left behind.

A small boat going from trawler to trawler to pick up men was soon loaded down.

Throughout the day and until darkness fell, they kept coming, more and more men, hugging, laughing, spilling onto the seven trawlers that were their ride out. Even just before the trawlers pushed off Benjina on the 24-hour trip to neighboring Tual island, fishermen were still running to the shore and clambering onto the vessels. Some were so sick and emaciated, they stumbled or had to be carried up the gang plank.

While excitement and relief flooded through many of the fishermen on the dock, others looked scared and unsure of what to expect next. Many complained they had no money to start over.

"I'm really happy, but I'm confused," said Nay Hla Win, 32. "I don't know what my future is in Myanmar."

Indonesian officials said security in Benjina is limited, with only two Navy officials stationed there to protect them. The men will be housed at a government compound while immigration is sorted out. Officials from Myanmar are set to visit the islands next week and will assist with bringing the men home and locating others.

The dramatic rescue came after a round of interviews Indonesian officials held with the fishermen, where they confirmed the abuse reported in the AP story, which included video of eight men locked in a cage and a slave graveyard. The men, mostly from Myanmar, talked of how they were beaten and shocked with Taser-like devices at sea, forced to work almost nonstop without clean water or proper food, paid little or nothing and prevented from going home.

Burmese fishermen prepare to board a boat during a rescue operation at the compound of Pusaka Benjina Resources fishing company, April 3, 2015. (AP Photo/Dita Alangkara)

There was essentially no way out: The island is so remote, there was no phone service until a cell tower was installed last month, and it is a difficult place to reach in the best of circumstances.

The abuse went even further at the hands of the man known as "the enforcer." This man, deeply feared and hated by the workers, was hired by their boat captains to punish them for misbehavior, they said.

Saw Eail Htoo and Myo Naing were among those he tormented. After three months at sea working with only two to four hours of sleep a night, the two Burmese slaves just wanted to rest. They fell asleep on the deck.

Their Thai captain decided to make an example of them, they said. So the two were driven by motorbike to a hill above the port. They were handcuffed together and placed in front of an Indonesian flag. Then they were punched in the face and kicked until they collapsed into the dirt, they said, blood oozing from their ripped faces.

Even then, the enforcer would not stop.

"He kept kicking me," said Naing, rail-thin with a military-style haircut. "I kept thinking, if I was at home, this wouldn't be happening."

The findings documented by Indonesian officials and the AP came in stark contrast to what a Thai delegation reported from a visit to Benjina earlier this week to find trafficked Thai nationals. They denied mistreatment on the boats and said the crews were all Thai, even though the AP found many migrant workers from other countries are issued fake documents with Thai names and addresses.

"We examined the boats and the crews, and the result is most of the crews are happy and a few of them are sick and willing to go home," said Thai police Lt. Gen. Saritchai Anekwiang, who was leading the delegation. "Generally, the boat conditions are good."

Thailand, the world's third-largest seafood exporter, has been under further pressure to clean up its industry since the AP tracked slave-caught seafood out of Benjina by satellite and linked it to the supply chains of some of America's largest supermarkets and retailers. The U.S. State Department said Friday that it is pressing Myanmar to quickly repatriate the men. U.S. retailers also called for action and commended Indonesian officials.

"We don't condone human trafficking in the supply chain, and we applaud the government's work to end this abuse. Our hearts go out to these men, and we wish them well on their journeys home," said Wal-Mart spokeswoman Marilee McInnis.

Last week, the International Organization for Migration said there could be as many as 4,000 foreign men, many trafficked or enslaved, who are stranded on islands surrounding Benjina following a fishing moratorium called by the Indonesian Fisheries Ministry to crack down on poaching. Indonesia has some of the world's richest fishing grounds, and the government estimates billions of dollars in seafood are stolen from its waters by foreign crews every year.

Three-quarters of the more than 320 migrant workers who left the island on Friday were Burmese, but about 50 from the country refused to go, saying they had not received their salaries and did not want leave without money.

Some were also from Cambodia and Laos. A few Thais were allowed to board the boats, but the Indonesians said Thai nationals could stay on Benjina more safely, since Thai captains were less likely to abuse them.

Burmese fishermen carry their belongings as they wait for their departure to leave the compound of Pusaka Benjina Resources fishing company, April 3, 2015. (AP Photo/Dita Alangkara)

"I expected to evacuate all of them, but I did not expect it this soon," said Ida Kusuma, one of the leaders of the Fisheries Ministry delegation. "But I think it's good."

Police are investigating in Benjina and will decide whether to prosecute those involved in abuse, said Kedo Arya, head of Maluku province prosecutor's office. The Indonesian officials were told "the enforcer" was being detained.

For those like Naing, who recalled being tortured, beaten and locked in a room for a month and 17 days for simply falling asleep, the thought of finally leaving the island was impossible to believe.

"Is it real that we are going home?" he asked.

A firework soon shot off from one of the boats, signaling it was indeed time to go. The same trawlers where the fishermen had suffered years of abuse were heading back to sea. This time crowded with free men full of hope.

MORE THAN 300 SLAVE FISHERMEN NOW SAFE
Tual, Indonesia, Saturday, April 4, 2015

The same trawlers that had enslaved countless migrant fishermen for years carried more than 300 of them to freedom Saturday, following a dramatic rescue from a remote Indonesian island that many men believed would likely be their final resting place.

After 17 hours overnight at sea, the men, mostly from Myanmar, took their first steps of freedom. They filed off the boats and walked to the site of their new temporary home where they were finally safe.

They moved in an orderly, single-file line with colored ribbons tied around their wrists to identify which of the six vessels had brought them. They were tired from the long, cramped journey, but smiled and laughed while talking about the new lives they were about to start. At one point, a group sang and clapped their hands. But mostly, the fear of being beaten or killed by their captors had finally lifted.

"I'm so happy, I wanted to go home for so long," said Aung Aung, 26, who lifted his hair on the left side of his head to show a fat, jagged scar stretching from his lip to the back of his neck - the result of a machete attack by his captain's son. "I missed home and especially after I was cut ... I was afraid I would die there."

The Burmese men were among hundreds of migrant workers revealed in an Associated Press investigation to have been lured or tricked into leaving their countries to go to Thailand, where they were put on boats and brought to Indonesia. From there, they were forced to catch seafood that was shipped back to Thailand and exported to consumers around the world, including the United States. In response to the AP's findings, an Indonesian delegation visited the island village of Benjina on Friday and offered immediate evacuation after finding brutal conditions, down to an "enforcer" paid to beat men up.

The officials from the Fisheries Ministry offered the men a chance to leave, fearing they would not be safe if they stayed on the island after speaking out about the horrendous labor abuses they endured.

About 320 men took up the offer. Even as a downpour started, some dashed through the rain. They sprinted back to their boats, jumped over the rails and threw themselves through windows. They stuffed their meager belongings into plastic bags, small suitcases and day packs, and rushed back to the dock, not wanting to be left behind.

After arriving on the island of Tual on Saturday afternoon, the men were given traditional packets of Indonesian rice wrapped in paper. Those who were sick or injured were offered medical care by paramedics inside ambulances.

The ministry has expressed some concern over how to feed so many people for an extended period of time, but a large open-air pavilion is being provided for the men to sleep under. The accommodation is crude with a concrete floor, but it has a roof to keep them dry and, most importantly, they are safe.

Officials from Myanmar are set to visit the islands next week and will assist with bringing the men home and locating others who are still trapped.

Friday's unexpected rescue came after a round of interviews Indonesian officials held with the fishermen, where they confirmed the abuse reported in the AP story, which included video of eight migrants locked in a cage and a slave graveyard. The men talked of how they were beaten and shocked with Taser-like devices at sea, forced to work almost nonstop without clean water or proper food, paid little or nothing and prevented from going home.

Recently rescued Burmese fishermen smile on their boat upon arrival in Tual, April 4, 2015. (AP Photo/Dita Alangkara)

There was essentially no way out. Benjina is in the far reaches of Indonesia and so remote, there was no phone service until a cell tower was installed last month, and it is a difficult place to reach in the best of circumstances.

Some of the men said the abuse went even further at the hands of an Indonesian man known as "the enforcer." He was deeply feared and hated by the workers, who said he was hired by their boat captains to punish them for misbehavior.

The findings documented by Indonesian officials and the AP came in stark contrast to what a Thai delegation reported from a visit to Benjina earlier this week when they searched for trafficked Thai nationals. They denied mistreatment on the boats and said the crews were all Thai, even though the AP found many migrant workers from other countries were issued fake documents with Thai names and addresses.

Thailand, the world's third-largest seafood exporter, has been under further pressure to clean up its industry since the AP tracked a boat of slave-caught seafood by satellite from Benjina to a port outside of Bangkok. Records then linked it to the supply chains of some of America's largest supermarkets and retailers and among the most popular brands of pet foods.

The U.S. State Department said Friday that it is pressing Myanmar to quickly repatriate the men. U.S. companies also called for action and commended Indonesian officials.

"We don't condone human trafficking in the supply chain, and we applaud the government's work to end this abuse. Our hearts go out to these men, and we wish them well on their journeys home," said Marilee McInnis, spokeswoman for Wal-Mart, the largest retailer in the U.S., which was among those the AP found with supply chains linked to tainted seafood.

The International Organization for Migration has said there could be as many as 4,000 foreign men, many trafficked or enslaved, who are stranded on islands surrounding Benjina following a fishing moratorium called by the Indonesian Fisheries Ministry to crack down on poaching. The country has some of the world's richest fishing grounds, and the government estimates billions of dollars in seafood are stolen from its waters by foreign crews every year.

Three-quarters of the more than 320 migrant workers who left the island on Friday were Burmese. Others were also from Cambodia and Laos, and a few Thais were allowed to board the boats. However, the Indonesians said most Thai nationals could stay on Benjina more safely, since Thai captains were less likely to abuse them.

Many of the men hugged and jumped in the air when they learned they were finally leaving the island, but others worry it will be difficult to readjust to the countries they left behind.

Phong Myant Aung, 37, worked on a trawler for six years and said he was constantly physically and verbally abused and not given medicine when he got sick.

His face lit up when asked how he felt as a free man. But when the question turned to what he would do when he returned to Myanmar, his eyes slowly filled with tears and he struggled to find words.

"I really don't know. I have no education," he said, pausing to wipe his cheek. "My parents are old, I want to be with them."

Burmese fishermen hug each other as they wait for their departure to leave the compound of Pusaka Benjina Resources fishing company in Benjina, April 3, 2015. (AP Photo/Dita Alangkara)

FIRST ONES HOME BUT HUNDREDS WAITING
Tual, Indonesia, Wednesday, May 13, 2015

When Kyaw Naing arrived at the tiny thatch-and-bamboo shack in Myanmar, it was empty and the door stood wide open.

He was finally home, after five years of being forced to work as a slave on a fishing boat, but there was no one to greet him. His brother - and only living relative - was gone.

Kyaw Naing, 30, who was kept at one point in a cage on the remote Indonesian island village of Benjina, is among eight migrant fishermen rescued for their safety during an Associated Press investigation into slavery in the seafood industry. Those men are now home, and hundreds more are waiting to be repatriated after the Indonesian government evacuated them to another island following the story's publication.

Kyaw Naing, right, a former slave fishermen rests at a Myanmar government's welfare center upon his return to Yangon. He was among the first Burmese men to return home following an Associated Press investigation into the use of forced labor in the Thai seafood industry, May 9, 2015. (AP Photo/Gemunu Amarasinghe)

The number of former slaves found has risen steadily in the past month to nearly 600, reflecting how widespread and deep-rooted the problem of forced labor is on the boats that bring them from Thailand. Before the first men left to go home this week, more than 360 were gathered on the island of Tual, including some who got word of the rescue and traveled hundreds of miles by boat to join the others. Another 230 Burmese and Cambodians have been identified and are waiting to leave Benjina, while hundreds of Thai nationals still have not been processed there.

In addition, the AP recently found more foreign migrants desperate to go home during a visit to the provincial capital of Ambon. The International Organization for Migration suspects thousands of others are stranded on boats or surrounding islands.

A rescue is what Kyaw Naing hoped for when he agreed to talk on camera through the rusty bars of his cage in November. He said he had been locked up by his Thai captain for asking to go home.

"I was really upset because I didn't know when I was going to return. When I looked at the sea, all I saw was water - ocean all over. I was hopeless," he said. "I did the video and volunteered it to let the whole world know."

In this Monday, April 6, 2015 photo, former fishing slave Kyaw Naing pauses during an interview with the Associated Press in Jakarta, Indonesia, April 6, 2015. (AP Photo/Dita Alangkara)

Most of the men are from Myanmar, also known as Burma, but some are from Cambodia, Laos and poor parts of Thailand. They were sold, tricked or even kidnapped in Thailand and brought to work in Indonesian waters for little or no pay. They were forced to work up to 24 hours a day with inadequate food and unclean water, and many reported being beaten and denied medical care.

The AP linked their catch to the supply chains of some of America's biggest food sellers, such as Wal-Mart, Sysco and Kroger, and also to popular brands of canned pet food, including Fancy Feast, Meow Mix and Iams. The companies have all said they strongly condemn labor abuse and are taking steps to prevent it, such as working with human rights groups to hold subcontractors accountable.

On Monday, 59 former slaves from Cambodia became the first to return home there. Sim Chhorn, 69, traveled to the airport from the central part of the county to meet her son.

"I thought in this life, I would not see him again," she said with a quivering voice before their reunion.

The hundreds of men still waiting at the port in Tual are now free to relax and laugh as they kick a rattan ball over a net in the traditional Burmese game of "chinlone." Some watch the sunset at dusk or lounge in hammocks listening to Burmese music. Others sit in the cool grass of an open field getting haircuts.

But significant challenges remain, including the cost of feeding them, providing medical care and getting them home.

Repatriation is expensive due to air travel. Australia has already donated more than $1.6 million, while the U.S. paid $35,000 for the Cambodians' flights and has provided another $225,000 to support case workers, health care, food, water and shelter. Myanmar is planning chartered flights, the first of which is scheduled for Thursday, and the IOM has been coordinating efforts and providing other necessities.

Much more is needed, especially since many of the fishermen were paid little or nothing and are going home penniless. Some have not been in contact with family for years and aren't sure if relatives have moved or even if they will find them alive.

"The overall response so far is a good first step in tackling human trafficking in the fishing industry that has been allowed to run rampant for far too long," said Steve Hamilton, deputy chief of mission at the IOM in Indonesia. "But it is only a first step of many that need to follow."

In the meantime, authorities in Indonesia and Thailand are working to punish those responsible.

On Tuesday, Indonesian police announced the first arrests in the case. Two Indonesian employees of Pusaka Benjina Resources, one of the largest fishing companies in eastern Indonesia, and five Thai captains were taken into custody on charges of human trafficking. Authorities have vowed more arrests will follow, and the country's Human Rights Commission is investigating.

Meanwhile, Jakarta police said Wednesday that a Fisheries Ministry official from Benjina who was slated to be a key witness had died of a heart attack. The Fisheries minister has launched an internal investigation, and other witnesses have been placed in protection.

Thailand's prime minister's office has also said it is probing the Benjina case.

"I am surprised and saddened," said Myanmar police Lt. Col. Khin Maung Hla, who visited the Indonesian islands last month to investigate the problem. "I think the Thai companies should be held responsible because they are the ones bringing these people overseas."

Kyaw Naing, left, a former slave fishermen, is questioned by officials after arriving in Yangon, Myanmar, May 9, 2015. (AP Photo/Khin Maung Win)

However, Wiriya Sirichaiekawat, vice chair of the National Fisheries Association of Thailand, said that the problems are not representative of the entire Thai fishing industry. He added that he doesn't believe many of the men from Benjina were unpaid.

"Maybe 1 percent," he said of the level of labor abuses aboard Thai boats in foreign waters. "Not all of them."

Kyaw Naing insists he is still owned for years of work on his boat. Now that he's back home in Myanmar's Irrawaddy Delta, he realizes the chances of ever receiving any wages are slim. But for now, he has something better than money.

After waiting for a while at the little hut, his older brother finally returned. Kyaw Naing immediately approached and knelt before him, offering respect according to the country's Buddhist tradition.

There were no dramatic hugs or tears. But both men smiled as the younger brother told an edited version of his life on the high seas - minus the slavery and despair - and talked about his dream of opening a barber shop in Myanmar.

"Whether he is rich or poor, I am so happy to see him again," said Kyaw Oo, who happily opened his family's 8-foot by 8-foot home to the brother he thought he'd lost. "After all these years, I wondered if he had forgotten me. Or does he still recognize me as a brother? Or is he dead or alive?"

NEW ROUND OF SLAVE RESCUES
Friday, July 31, 2015

Authorities in Papua New Guinea have rescued eight fishermen held on board a Thai-owned refrigerated cargo ship, and dozens of other boats are still being sought in response to an Associated Press report that included satellite photos and locations of slave vessels at sea.

Two Burmese and six Cambodian men have been removed from the Blissful Reefer, a massive quarter-acre transport ship now impounded in Daru, Papua New Guinea, about 120 miles (200 kilometers) north of Australia. Officials said the fishermen appeared to be part of a larger group of forced laborers being transported from Thailand to be distributed onto various fishing boats, said George Gigauri, head of the International Organization for Migration in Port Moresby, which has assisted with the operation. He added that nearly 20 other crewmembers from the Blissful Reefer have not yet been questioned, and that if victims of trafficking are found, "there are lives at risk."

Former Burmese slave fishermen Kaung Htet Wai, left and Lin Lin, second right, at home in Yangon, Myanmar, look at satellite images showing two trawlers loading fish onto a giant refrigerated cargo ship in waters off Papua New Guinea. They spent months in the same waters loading fish onto ships owned by the Thai Silver Sea Fishery Company, July 1, 2015. (AP Photo/Gemunu Amarasinghe)

The men are part of a seemingly inexhaustible supply of poor migrants from Myanmar, Cambodia and Laos who are forced to fish for the Thai seafood industry. When workers run away, become sick or even die, they are easily replaced by new recruits who are tricked or coerced by false promises of jobs in Thailand.

The story of Aung San Win, 19, who was among the rescued men, started the same way as with hundreds of other enslaved fishermen interviewed in person or in writing by AP during a year-long investigation into slavery at sea. He said a broker came to his home in Myanmar and convinced him and several other young men to go to Thailand where they could find good work in factories. But when they arrived, their passports and identification cards were taken. They were then pushed onto boats and told they would have to fish for three years and owed nearly $600 for their documents, he said.

Soe Lay, 20, who worked in a shrimp shed in Samut Sakhon, Thailand. He says he could not leave because his migrant passport was taken by the shed's owner, and that he was once taken to the police station for stealing six pieces of shrimp to eat from the shed, August 31, 2015. (AP Photo/Esther Htusan)

"They told us that we have to get off in this place and work here," said Aung, who added that it had taken about 20 days to reach Papua New Guinea, after stops in Singapore and Australia. "I don't want to work here. I don't even know what this place is."

Enslaved fishermen are routinely hauled from Thailand to work on smaller Thai trawlers in foreign waters where they are given little or no pay. Hundreds of former slaves told AP they were beaten or witnessed other crew members being attacked. They were routinely denied medicine, forced to work 22-hour shifts with no days off and given inadequate food and impure water.

The ship seized in Papua New Guinea, the Blissful Reefer, appears to be connected to a trafficking ring exposed by the AP that was sending seafood caught by slaves around the Indonesian island of Benjina to the United States. The Blissful Reefer is listed by Indonesian authorities as one of nine massive seafood transporters chartered by the fishing company in Benjina. And documents from the men on board showed they were brought to work on two trawlers, Chainavee 12 and Chainavee 24, from the same family of vessels AP found in Benjina.

The AP investigation revealed fishermen being held in a cage, buried under fake names in a company graveyard and trapped for years with no way to return home. Journalists followed their slave-caught fish back to Thailand and linked it to the supply chains of major U.S. food sellers, such as Wal-Mart, Sysco and Kroger, and American pet food companies, including Fancy Feast, Meow Mix and Iams. The businesses have all said they strongly condemn labor abuse and vowed to take steps to prevent it.

The report prompted rescues and repatriation of more than 800 men, and seven people have been charged with human trafficking.

In the past four months, AP has been tracking down another 34 boats, with as many as 20 men aboard each, that fled the slave island well before authorities and investigators arrived. First-hand accounts, satellite photos and public records located at least some of the vessels in a narrow, dangerous strait in western Papua New Guinea.

Authorities there then searched the fishing grounds, called the dogleg, with aircraft and stopped the Blissful Reefer. The prime minister's office in Papua New Guinea and the National Fisheries Authority did not respond to requests for comment.

Indonesia Fisheries Minister Susi Pudjiastuti, whose investigators had been chasing the boats from Benjina, said she has asked Papua New Guinea to send back any illegal trawlers that fled her country for prosecution.

International Organization for Migration spokesman Leonard Doyle told a United Nations briefing in Geneva that AP had alerted authorities last week about suspect boats and searchers had found "a group of mariners from one of these vessels to be victims of trafficking." But time is ticking to find the others. All foreign boats must leave the Papua New Guinea strait by Friday, when a fishing moratorium will be put in place to clamp down on poaching, according to the National Fisheries Authority.

A patrol boat is expected to be sent to search waters in the strait along with a surveillance plane, Gigauri said. The eight men aboard the Blissful Reefer will be returned home.

2,000 AND COUNTING
Ambon, Indonesia, Tuesday, September 17, 2015

More than 2,000 fishermen have been rescued this year from brutal conditions at sea, liberated as a result of an Associated Press investigation into seafood brought to the U.S. from a slave island in eastern Indonesia.

Dozens of Burmese men in the bustling port town of Ambon were the latest to go home, some more than a decade after being trafficked onto Thai trawlers. Grabbing one another's hands, the men walked together toward buses last week. As they pulled away for the airport, some of those still waiting their turn to go home cheered, throwing their arms in the air.

"I'm sure my parents think I'm dead," said Tin Lin Tun, 25, who lost contact with his family after a broker lured him to Thailand five years ago. Instead of working in construction, as promised, he was sold onto a fishing boat and taken to Indonesia. "I'm their only son. They're going to cry so hard when they see me."

The reunion he envisions has played out hundreds of times since March, after the AP tracked fish - caught by men who were savagely beaten and caged - to the supply chains of some of America's biggest food sellers, such as Wal-Mart, Sysco and Kroger, and popular brands of canned pet food like Fancy Feast, Meow Mix and Iams. It can turn up as calamari at fine restaurants, as imitation crab in a sushi roll or as packages of frozen snapper relabeled with store brands that land on our dinner tables. The U.S. companies have all said they strongly condemn labor abuse and are taking steps to prevent it.

In response, a multimillion-dollar Thai-Indonesian fishing business has been shut down, at least nine people have been arrested and two fishing cargo vessels have been seized. In the U.S., importers have demanded change, three class-action lawsuits are underway, new laws have been introduced and the Obama administration is pushing exporters to clean up their labor practices. The AP's work was entered into the congressional record for a hearing, and is scheduled to be brought up for discussion again later this month.

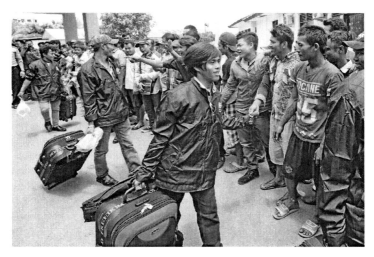

Burmese fishermen bid goodbye to their friends as they leave the port town of Ambon, September 8, 2015. (AP Photo/Achmad Ibrahim)

The largest impact, by far, has been the rescue of some of the most desperate and isolated people in the world. More than 2,000 men from Myanmar, Thailand, Cambodia and Laos have been identified or repatriated since the AP's initial story ran, according to the International Organization for Migration and foreign ministries. The tally includes eight fishermen trafficked aboard a Thai cargo ship seized in neighboring Papua New Guinea.

And those returnee figures don't tell the whole story: Hundreds more have been quietly sent home by their companies, avoiding human trafficking allegations.

"We've never seen a rescue on this scale before," said Lisa Rende Taylor, an anti-trafficking expert formerly with the United Nations who now heads the anti-slavery nonprofit Project Issara. "They deserve compensation and justice."

Many experts believe the most effective pressure for change can come from consumers, whose hunger for cheap seafood is helping fuel the massive labor abuses. Southeast Asia's fishing industry is dominated by Thailand, which earns $7 billion annually in exports. The business relies on tens of thousands of poor migrant laborers, mainly from neighboring Southeast Asian countries. They often are tricked, sold or kidnapped and put onto boats that are commonly sent to distant foreign waters to poach fish.

A year-long investigation led the AP to the island village of Benjina, part of Indonesia's Maluku chain about 400 miles north of Australia. There, workers considered runaway risks were padlocked behind the rusty bars of a cage.

Men in Benjina - both those stuck on Thai fishing boats and others who had escaped into the jungle - were the first to go home when rescues led by the Indonesian government began in early April. Since then, hundreds more have been identified and repatriated from neighboring islands. Many of those leaving recently from Ambon were handed cash payments by company officials, but they said the money was a fraction of what they were owed.

An AP survey of almost 400 men underscores the horrific conditions fishing slaves faced. Many described being whipped with stingray tails, deprived of food and water and forced to work for years without pay. More than 20 percent said they were beaten, 30 percent said they saw someone else beaten and 12 percent said they saw a person die.

"My colleague, Chit Oo, fell from the boat into the water," wrote Ye Aung, 32, of Myanmar. "The captain said there was no need to search, he will float by himself later."

Another man, 18-year-old Than Min Oo, said he was not paid and wrote simply: "Please help me."

For many, the return home is bittersweet. Parents collapse in tears upon seeing their sons, and some men meet siblings born after they left. But almost all come back empty-handed, struggle to find jobs and feel they are yet another burden to their extremely poor families. At least one crowd-sourcing site, set up by Anti-Slavery International, is aimed at helping them.

A study by the London School of Hygiene and Tropical Medicine earlier this year, based on interviews with over 1,000 trafficking survivors from different industries, found half of those returning from slavery at sea suffered from depression and around 40 percent from post-traumatic stress disorder or anxiety. Those men were not connected to the Benjina cases.

Former slave-fisherman Tun Lin, 33, is seen at a transit center in Yangon, Myanmar. One finger was ripped off while trying to wrangle an unwieldy net on the deck of his boat in eastern Indonesia, and the other three were crushed beyond saving, September 6, 2015. (AP Photo/Robin McDowell)

Many bear physical scars as well.

Tun Lin, who returned to Myanmar last week, held up his right hand: a stump with just a thumb.

He said one finger was ripped off while he tried to wrangle an unwieldy net on the deck of his boat, and the other three were crushed beyond saving. He was taken by refrigerated cargo delivery ship to Thailand, where the remaining digits were surgically removed. Four days later, he said, he was put back on a ship bound for Indonesia, where he fished for the next three years.

"There were some good captains, but there were a lot of bad ones," the 33-year-old said, his eyes filling with tears as he described how "boat leaders" were assigned to act as enforcers, beating up fishermen who weren't working fast enough. "When we asked for our money, they'd say they didn't have it ... but then they'd go to nightclubs, brothels and bars, drinking expensive alcohol."

Like many of the men rescued from Ambon, Tun Lin had been working for PT Mabiru Industries, where operations were halted several months ago as authorities investigated trafficking and illegal fishing in the industry there. Mabiru, one of more than a dozen fishing, processing and cold storage firms in Ambon, sold packages of yellowfin tuna largely headed for Japanese markets, and also shipped to the United States. The company is shuttered and its managers could not be reached.

Florida-based South Pacific Specialties, which distributes to supermarket chains, restaurants and food groups, received a shipping container loaded with frozen tuna from Mabiru in February. Managing partner Francisco Pinto told the AP his company had once rented out Mabiru's facilities in Ambon, bought tuna from private artisanal fishermen, and hired its own workers for filleting and processing fish. Pinto said he has spent the past six weeks in Indonesia meeting and observing fish suppliers because American customers are increasingly demanding fair treatment for workers.

Amid the increased scrutiny, some have taken legal action. In the past month, three separate class-action lawsuits have been filed naming Mars Inc., IAMS Co., Proctor & Gamble, Nestle USA Inc., Nestle Purina Petcare Co. and Costco, accusing them of having seafood supply chains tainted with slave labor. Ashley Klann, a spokeswoman for the Seattle-based law firm behind several of the cases, said the litigation "came as a result of AP's reporting."

Even with the increased global attention, hundreds of thousands of men still are forced to work in the seafood industry.

"Slavery in Southeast Asia's fishing industry is a real-life horror story," said Congressman Chris Smith, R-N.J., who is among those sponsoring new legislation. "It's no longer acceptable for companies to deny responsibility ... not when people are kept in cages, not when people are made to work like animals for decades to pad some company's bottom line."

Chapter 7

SHRIMP SLAVES

Female workers, wearing a yellow-white cosmetic paste known as thanka on their cheeks, sort shrimp at a seafood market in Mahachai, Thailand, September 3, 2015. (AP Photo/Gemunu Amarasinghe)

IS YOUR GROCER OR RESTAURANT SELLING YOU SLAVE-PEELED SHRIMP?
Samut Sakhon, Thailand, Tuesday, December 15, 2015

Every morning at 2 a.m., they heard a kick on the door and a threat: Get up or get beaten. For the next 16 hours, No. 31 and his wife stood in the factory that owned them with their aching hands in ice water. They ripped the guts, heads, tails and shells off shrimp bound for overseas markets, including grocery stores and all-you-can-eat buffets across the United States.

After being sold to the Gig Peeling Factory, they were at the mercy of their Thai bosses, trapped with nearly 100 other Burmese migrants. Children worked alongside them, including a girl so tiny she had to stand on a stool to reach the peeling table. Some had been there for months, even years, getting little or no pay. Always, someone was watching.

No names were ever used, only numbers given by their boss - Tin Nyo Win was No. 31.

Pervasive human trafficking has helped turn Thailand into one of the world's biggest shrimp providers. Despite repeated promises by businesses and government to clean up the country's $7 billion seafood export industry, an Associated Press investigation has found shrimp peeled by modern-day slaves is reaching the U.S., Europe and Asia.

The problem is fueled by corruption and complicity among police and authorities. Arrests and prosecutions are rare. Raids can end up sending migrants without proper paperwork to jail, while owners go unpunished.

More than 2,000 trapped fishermen have been freed this year as a result of an ongoing Associated Press investigative series into slavery in the Thai seafood industry. The reports also have led to a dozen arrests, millions of dollars' worth of seizures and proposals for new federal laws.

Hundreds of shrimp peeling sheds are hidden in plain sight on residential streets or behind walls with no signs in Samut Sakhon, a port town an hour outside Bangkok. The AP found one factory that was enslaving dozens of workers, and runaway migrants led rights groups to the Gig shed and a third facility. All three sheds held 50 to 100 people each, many locked inside.

As Tin Nyo Win soon found out for himself, there's no easy escape. One woman had been working at Gig for eight years. Another man ended up peeling shrimp there after breaking free from an equally brutal factory.

"I was shocked after working there a while, and I realized there was no way out," said Tin Nyo Win, 22, who has a baby face and teeth stained red from chewing betel nut.

Win Win Than, 25, who worked in a shrimp shed in Samut Sakhon, Thailand to pay off her 20,000 Baht (U.S. $550) debt even when she was pregnant. She said she tried to run away but was caught and handcuffed in a small room inside the shed, August 31, 2015. (AP Photo/Esther Htusan)

"I told my wife, 'We're in real trouble. If something ends up going wrong, we're going to die.'"

Last month, AP journalists followed and filmed trucks loaded with freshly peeled shrimp from the Gig shed to major Thai exporting companies and then, using U.S. customs records and Thai industry reports, tracked it globally. They also traced similar connections from another factory raided six months earlier, and interviewed more than two dozen workers from both sites.

U.S. customs records show the shrimp made its way into the supply chains of major U.S. food stores and retailers such as Wal-Mart, Kroger, Whole Foods, Dollar General and Petco, along with restaurants such as Red Lobster and Olive Garden.

It also entered the supply chains of some of America's best-known seafood brands and pet foods, including Chicken of the Sea and Fancy Feast, which are sold in grocery stores from Safeway and Schnucks to Piggly Wiggly and Albertsons. AP reporters went to supermarkets in all 50 states and found shrimp products from supply chains tainted with forced labor.

Female workers sort shrimp at a seafood market in Mahachai, Thailand, September 30, 2015. (AP Photo/Gemunu Amarasinghe)

European and Asian import and export records are confidential, but the Thai companies receiving shrimp tracked by the AP all say they ship to Europe and Asia as well.

The businesses that responded condemned the practices that lead to these conditions. Many said they were launching investigations when told their supply chains were linked to people held against their will in sheds like the Gig factory, which sat behind a gate off a busy street, between railroad tracks and a river.

Inside the large warehouse, toilets overflowed with feces, and the putrid smell of raw sewage wafted from an open gutter just outside the work area. Young children ran barefoot through suffocating dorm rooms. Entire families labored side-by-side at rows of stainless steel counters piled high with tubs of shrimp.

Tin Nyo Win and his wife, Mi San, were cursed for not peeling fast enough and called "cows" and "buffalos." They were allowed to go outside for food only if one of them stayed behind as insurance against running away.

But escaping was all they could think about.

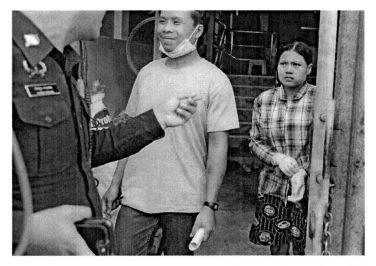

Burmese worker Tin Nyo Win, who was given the identification No. 31 at a shrimp shed where he and his wife worked, smiles as he is reunited with his wife Mi San in Samut Sakhon, Thailand, November 9, 2015. (AP Photo/Dita Alangkara)

Shrimp is the most-loved seafood in the U.S., with Americans downing 1.3 billion pounds every year, or about 4 pounds per person. Once a luxury reserved for special occasions, it became cheap enough for stir-fries and scampis when Asian farmers started growing it in ponds three decades ago. Thailand quickly dominated the market and now sends nearly half of its supply to the U.S.

The Southeast Asian country is one of the worst human trafficking hubs on earth. It has been blacklisted for the past two years by the U.S. State Department, which cited complicity by Thai officials. The European Union issued a warning earlier this year that tripled seafood import tariffs, and is expected to decide next month whether to impose an outright ban.

Consumers enjoy the convenience of dumping shrimp straight from freezer to skillet, the result of labor-intensive peeling and cleaning. Unable to keep up with demand, exporters get their supply from peeling sheds that are sometimes nothing more than crude garages adjacent to the boss's house. Supply chains are so complicated that, on any given day, buyers may not know exactly where the shrimp comes from.

The Thai Frozen Foods Association lists about 50 registered shrimp sheds in the country. However, hundreds more operate in Samut Sakhon, the country's main shrimp processing region. Here the humid air hangs thick with the smell of dead fish. Refrigerated trucks with seafood logos barrel down streets straddled by huge processing plants. Just as ubiquitous are the small pickups loaded with migrant workers from neighboring Cambodia, Laos and Myanmar being taken to gut, fillet, de-vein and peel the seafood that fuels this town's economy.

Shrimp are left on an abandoned peeling table as a Thai soldier walks past during a raid on the shrimp shed in Samut Sakhon, Thailand, November 9, 2015. (AP Photo/Dita Alangkara)

Abuse is common in Samut Sakhon. An International Labor Organization report estimated 10,000 migrant children aged 13 to 15 work in the city. Another U.N. agency study found nearly 60 percent of Burmese laborers toiling in its seafood processing industry were victims of forced labor.

Tin Nyo Win and his wife were taken to the Gig Peeling Factory in July when they made the long drive from Myanmar across the border, crammed so tightly into a truck with other workers that they could barely breathe. Like many migrants, they were lured from home by a broker with promises of good-paying jobs, and came without visas or work permits.

After being sold to the Gig shed, the couple learned they would have to work off what was considered their combined worth - $830. It was an insurmountable debt.

Because they were illegal workers, the owners constantly threatened to call police to keep them in line. Even documented migrants were vulnerable because the boss held onto identification papers so they could not leave.

Under the U.S. government's definition, forced labor and debt bondage are considered slavery.

In the Gig shed, employees' salaries were pegged to how fast their fingers could move. Tin Nyo Win and his wife peeled about 175 pounds of shrimp for just $4 a day, less than half of what they were promised. A female Thai manager, who slapped and cursed workers, often cut their wages without explanation. After they bought gloves and rubber boots, and paid monthly "cleaning fees" inside the trash-strewn shed, almost nothing was left.

Employees said they had to work even when they were ill. Seventeen children peeled alongside adults, sometimes crying, at stations where paint chipped off the walls and slick floors were eaten away by briny water.

Lunch breaks were only 15 minutes, and migrants were yelled at for talking too much. Several workers said a woman died recently because she didn't get proper medical care for her asthma. Children never went to school and began peeling shrimp just an hour later than adults.

"We had to get up at 3 in the morning and then start working continuously," said Eae Hpaw, 16, whose arms were a patchwork of scars from infections and allergies caused by the shrimp. "We stopped working around 7 in the evening. We would take a shower and sleep. Then we would start again."

After being roughed up one night by a supervisor, five months into their captivity, Tin Nyo Win and his wife decided they couldn't take the threats anymore.

Children and teenagers sit together to be registered by officials during a raid on a shrimp shed in Samut Sakhon, Thailand. Abuse is common in Samut Sakhon, which attracts workers from some of the world's poorest countries, mostly from Myanmar. An International Labor Organization report estimated 10,000 migrant children aged 13 to 15 work in the city, November 9, 2015. (AP Photo/Dita Alangkara)

"They would say, 'There's a gun in the boss's car and we're going to come and shoot you, and no one will know,'" he said.

The next morning, the couple saw an opportunity when the door wasn't being watched.

They ran.

Less than 24 hours later, Tin Nyo Win's wife was captured at a market by the shed manager. He watched helplessly as she was dragged away by her hair, terrified for her - and the baby they recently learned she was carrying.

Tracking shipments from just the Gig Peeling Factory highlights how fast and far slave-peeled shrimp can travel.

The AP followed trucks from the shed over five days to major Thai exporters. One load pulled into N&N Foods, owned by one of the world's largest seafood companies, Tokyo-based Maruha Nichiro Foods. A second drove to Okeanos Food, a subsidiary of another leading global seafood supplier, Thai Union. Still more went to Kongphop Frozen Foods and The Siam Union Frozen Foods, which have customers in the U.S., Canada, Europe, Asia and Australia. All the exporters and parent companies that responded said they abhor human rights abuses.

Burmese workers are escorted by soldiers and police officers as they leave a shrimp shed after a raid conducted by Thailand's Department of Special Investigation in Samut Sakhon, November 9, 2015. (AP Photo/Dita Alangkara)

Shrimp can mix with different batches of seafood as it is packaged, branded and shipped. At that point, there's no way to tell where any individual piece was peeled. Once it reaches American restaurants, hospitals, universities and military chow halls, all the shrimp from those four Thai processors is considered associated with slavery, according to United Nations and U.S. standards.

U.S. customs records linked the exported shrimp to more than 40 U.S. brands, including popular names such as Sea Best, Waterfront Bistro and Aqua Star. The AP found shrimp products with the same labels in more than 150 stores across America - from Honolulu to New York City to a tiny West Virginia town of 179 people. The grocery store chains have tens of thousands of U.S. outlets where millions of Americans shop.

In addition, the Thai distributors state on their websites that they export to Europe and Asia, although specific records are confidential. AP reporters in Germany, Italy, England and Ireland researched shrimp in supermarkets and found several brands sourced from Thailand. Those stores said the names of their Thai distributors are proprietary. Royal Greenland - an importer whose shrimp was seen under store brands as a product from Thailand but has not been linked to the sheds - said it now has shifted its sourcing to Ecuador.

By all accounts, the work at the Gig shed was off the books - and thus even businesses carefully tracking the provenance of the shrimp called the AP's findings a surprise.

"I want to eliminate this," said Dirk Leuenberger, CEO of Aqua Star. "I think it's disgusting that it's even remotely part of my business."

Some, including Red Lobster, Whole Foods and H-E-B Supermarkets, said they were confident - based on assurances from their Thai supplier - that their particular shrimp was not associated with abusive factories. That Thai supplier admits it hadn't known where it was getting all its shrimp and sent a note outlining corrective measures to U.S. businesses demanding answers last week.

"I am deeply disappointed that despite our best efforts we have discovered this potential instance of illegal labor practice in our supply chain," Thai Union CEO Thiraphong Chansiri wrote. His statement acknowledged "that illicitly sourced product may have fraudulently entered its supply chain" and confirmed a supplier "was doing business with an unregistered pre-processor in violation of our code of conduct."

After AP brought its findings to dozens of global retailers, Thai Union announced it will bring all shrimp-processing in-house by the end of the year and provide jobs to workers whose factories close as a result. It's a significant step from the industry leader whose international brands include John West in Britain, Petit Navire in France and Mareblu in Italy; shrimp from abusive factories in Thailand has not been associated with them.

Susan Coppedge, the U.S. State Department's new anti-trafficking ambassador, said problems persist because brokers, boat captains and seafood firms aren't held accountable and victims have no recourse.

Susan Coppedge, the U.S. State Department's new anti-trafficking ambassador, speaks about slavery in the seafood industry during an interview in her office in Washington, November 20, 2015. (AP Photo/Carolyn Kaster)

"We have told Thailand to improve their anti-trafficking efforts, to increase their prosecutions, to provide services to victims," she said. She added that American consumers "can speak through their wallets and tell companies: 'We don't want to buy things made with slavery.'"

The State Department has not slapped Thailand with sanctions applied to other countries with similarly weak human trafficking records because it is a strategically critical Southeast Asian ally. And federal authorities say they can't enforce U.S. laws that ban importing goods produced by forced labor, citing an exception for items consumers can't get from another source. Thai shrimp slips right through that loophole.

Thailand is not the only source of slave-tainted seafood in the U.S., where nearly 90 percent of shrimp is imported.

The State Department's annual anti-trafficking reports have tied such seafood to 55 countries on six continents, including major suppliers to the U.S. Earlier this year, the AP uncovered a slave island in Benjina, Indonesia, where hundreds of migrant fishermen were trafficked from Thailand and sometimes locked in a cage. Last month, food giant Nestle disclosed that its own Thai suppliers were abusing and enslaving workers and has vowed to force change.

Human trafficking in Thailand also stretches far beyond the seafood industry. Earlier this year, high-ranking officials were implicated in a smuggling syndicate involving tens of thousands of Rohingya Muslims fleeing persecution in Myanmar. A crackdown came after dozens of victims died in Thai jungle camps because they were unable to pay ransoms.

The junta military government has singled out the country's fisheries sector for reforms. It says it has passed new laws to crack down on illegal activities aboard fishing boats and inside seafood-processing factories and is working to register undocumented migrant workers.

"There have been some flaws in the laws, and we have been closing those gaps," said M.L. Puntarik Smiti, the Thai Labor Ministry's permanent secretary. "The government has made human trafficking a national agenda. The policy is clear, and every department is working in the same direction. ... In the past, most punishments focused on the laborers, but now more focus is put on punishing the employers."

Police point to a new law that goes after officers involved in human trafficking, and say rooting out corruption and complicity is a priority.

Critics argue, however, the changes have been largely cosmetic. Former slaves repeatedly described how police took them into custody and then sold them to agents who trafficked them again into the seafood industry.

"There are laws and regulations, but they are being selectively enforced to benefit one side," said Patima Tungpuchayakul, manager of the Thai-based nonprofit Labor Rights Promotion Network Foundation. "When you find there is a child working 16 hours a day and getting paid ($2.75) ... the government has to put a stop to this."

The peeling sheds that supply to major Thai seafood companies are supposed to be certified and inspected, but the stamp of approval does not always prevent abuses.

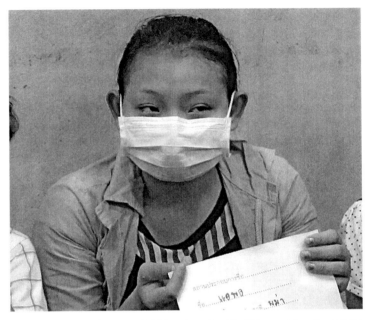

Eae Hpaw, 16, an undocumented child worker, sits with children and teenagers as she is registered by officials during a raid on a shrimp shed in Samut Sakhon, Thailand, November 9, 2015. (AP Photo/Dita Alangkara)

A factory just a few miles away from Tin Nyo Win's shed provided shrimp to companies including Thai Union; a half-dozen former workers said a Thai Union employee visited the shed every day. A runaway worker alerted a local migrant labor group about slave-like conditions there after being brutally beaten across his ear and throat with iron chains. Police raided the factory in May.

Former employees told the AP they had been locked inside and forced to work long hours with no days off and little sleep.

The conditions they described inside were horrific: A woman eight months pregnant miscarried on the shed floor and was forced to keep peeling for four days while hemorrhaging. An unconscious toddler was refused medical care after falling about 12 feet onto a concrete floor. Another pregnant woman escaped only to be tracked down, yanked into a car by her hair and handcuffed to a fellow worker at the factory.

"Sometimes when we were working, the tears would run down our cheeks because it was so tiring we couldn't bear it," said the worker who ran away. His name is being withheld due to concerns about his safety.

"We were crying, but we kept peeling shrimp," he said. "We couldn't rest. ... I think people are guilty if they eat the shrimp that we peeled like slaves."

Shrimp from that factory entered the supply chains of Thai Union, which, in the six months prior to the bust, shipped 15 million pounds of frozen shrimp to dozens of U.S. companies, customs records show. Those included Red Lobster and Darden Restaurants, which owns outlets such as Olive Garden, LongHorn Steakhouse and several other popular American chains.

Shrimp products from Thailand packaged under the name "Waterfront Bistro" at a Safeway grocery store in Phoenix. Despite Thailand's repeated promises to clean up in its $7 billion seafood export industry, little has changed, November 30 2015. (AP Photo/Ross D. Franklin)

The runaway worker was a free man after the May raid. But five months later, running low on cash with a pregnant wife, he felt desperate enough to look for a job in another shrimp factory. He hoped conditions would be better this time.

They weren't. His wages were withheld, and he ended up in the Gig factory peeling shrimp next to Tin Nyo Win - No. 31.

Modern-day slavery is often just part of doing business in Thailand's seafood export capital. Some shed owners believe they are providing jobs to poor migrant workers in need. Police are paid to look the other way and say officers frequently do not understand that practices such as forced labor and debt bondage are against the law.

"We just need to educate everyone on this issue," said Jaruwat Vaisaya, deputy commissioner of Bangkok's Metropolitan Police. "I don't think they know what they're doing is called human trafficking, but they must know it's wrong."

News surfaces about an abusive shed only when workers become so hopeless they're willing to risk everything to escape. Once on the street, without documentation, they are in some ways even more vulnerable. They face possible arrest and deportation or being resold.

After fleeing the Gig shed, Tin Nyo Win was alone. He didn't even know where the shed manager had taken his wife. He sought help from a local labor rights group, which prompted police to take action.

At dawn on Nov. 9, nearly two weeks after running away, he returned to the shed wearing dark glasses, a hat and a mask to keep the owners from recognizing him. He burst through the gate with dozens of officers and military troops, and frantically searched for his wife in the dim quarters on both floors of the maze-like complex.

Frightened Burmese workers huddled on the dirty concrete floor, the men and women separated. Some could be heard whispering: "That's 31. He came back." One young mother breast-fed a 5-month-old baby, while 17 children were taken to a corner.

Tin Nyo Win's wife was nowhere.

With law enforcement leading the way, it didn't take long to find her, though: Mi San was at a nearby fish factory. After being caught by the shed manager, she was taken to police. But instead of treating her as a trafficking victim, she said they put her back to work. Even as police and her husband escorted her out of the second factory, the Thai owner followed them into the street, complaining that Mi San still owed $22 for the pork and chicken she ate.

Burmese worker Tin Nyo Win, who is known as No. 31, right, helps remove a pair of gloves from the hands of his wife, Mi San, during their reunion in Samut Sakhon, Thailand, November 9, 2015. (AP Photo/Dita Alangkara)

For Thai police, it looked like a victory in front of the cameras. But the story does not end there.

No one at the Gig shed was arrested for human trafficking, a law that's seldom enforced. Instead, migrants with papers, including seven children, were sent back there to work. Another 10 undocumented children were taken from their parents and put into a shelter, forced to choose between staying there for years or being deported back to Myanmar alone. Nineteen other illegal workers were detained.

Tin Nyo Win and his wife soon found out that not even whistleblowers are protected. Just four days after being reunited, the couple was fingerprinted and locked inside a Thai jail cell without even a mattress. They were held on nearly $4,000 bail and charged with entering the country illegally and working without permits.

Back at the shed where their nightmare began, a worker reached by phone pleaded for help as trucks loaded with slave-peeled shrimp continued to roll out.

Burmese shrimp shed worker Tin Nyo Win, left, and his wife, Mi San, stand in a jail cell after they were arrested in Samut Sakhon. Even after Tin Nyo Win became a whistle-blower against the shrimp shed where they worked, the couple was fingerprinted and held on nearly $4,000 bail and charged with entering the country illegally and working without permits, November 13, 2015. (AP Photo/Robin McDowell)

AFTERMATH

The Gig Peeling Factory is now closed, with workers moved to another shed linked to the same owners, said Chaiyuth Thomya, the superintendent of Samut Sakhon's main police station. A Gig owner reached by phone by the AP declined to comment.

Jaruwat, the Bangkok police official, was alerted to how the case was being handled and has ordered local authorities to re-investigate it for human trafficking, and arrests have since been made. Tin Nyo Win and his pregnant wife were released from jail 10 days after they were locked up and are now being housed in a government shelter for victims of human trafficking.

Chaiyuth called a meeting to explain human trafficking laws to nearly 60 shed owners, some of whom were confused about raids that swept up illegal migrants. Later, Chaiyuth quoted one shed owner as saying, "I'm not selling drugs, why did they take possession of my things?"

Meanwhile, the AP informed labor rights investigators who work closely with police about another shed where workers said they were being held against their will. It is being examined.

CALL FOR BOYCOTT OF SLAVE-PEELED SHRIMP
New York, Tuesday, December 15, 2015

U.S. officials and human rights activists called on Americans to stop buying fish and shrimp tied to supply chains in Thailand, where The Associated Press has found slaves are forced to work in the seafood industry.

"All of us may find ourselves eating a slave-made product without knowing it, but once we know it, we all have a moral obligation, I believe, to make a personal decision to boycott it," said New Jersey Republican Congressman Chris Smith, a member of the House Foreign Relations Committee.

Rep. Chris Smith, R-N.J., speaks with an Associated Press reporter in his office on Capitol Hill in Washington. Human rights activists and U.S. officials, including Smith, called on Americans to stop buying fish and shrimp tied to supply chains in Thailand, November 20, 2015. (AP Photo/Carolyn Kaster)

Said Mark Lagon, president of the group Freedom House: "This isn't a matter of low pay or crummy working conditions. This isn't a matter of saving lots of money to choose the product that is made by cutting corners. This is the flagrant abuse of fellow human beings ... Americans won't stand for that."

The AP reported Monday that it found enslaved workers who were forced to peel shrimp in Thailand for up to 16 hours a day for little or no pay, and many were locked inside for months or even years on end. Journalists followed trucks from an abusive factory raided last month to major Thai distributors, and traced similar connections from another factory raided in May.

U.S. customs records show the shrimp made its way into the supply chains of major U.S. food stores and retailers such as Wal-Mart, Kroger, Dollar General and Petco, along with restaurants such as Olive Garden.

It also entered the supply chains of some of America's best-known seafood brands and pet foods, including Chicken of the Sea and Fancy Feast, which are sold in grocery stores from Safeway and

Schnucks to Piggly Wiggly and Albertsons. AP reporters went to supermarkets in all 50 states and found shrimp products from supply chains tainted with forced labor.

The businesses that responded condemned the practices that lead to these conditions. Many said they were launching investigations.

Responding to the AP reports, Red Lobster, Whole Foods and some others said they've been assured by their supplier, Thai Union, that their particular shrimp were not processed by children and slaves, despite the AP's findings.

Thai Union, meanwhile, admitted it hadn't known the source of all its shrimp, and sent a note outlining corrective measures to U.S. businesses. "We were concerned that, despite regular audits, it is difficult to guarantee that all external pre-processors were adhering to our code of conduct," Thai Union CEO Thiraphong Chansiri said in a statement.

President and CEO of Thai Union Group, Thiraphong Chansiri gestures during an interview at his company offices in Bangkok, Thailand. The president of Thailand's seafood giant expressed frustration and promised change after confirming that shrimp peeled by slaves was entering his company's supply chain, saying he would end reliance on poorly regulated contractors responsible for the abuses, December 15, 2015. (AP Photo/Mark Baker)

The company promised to exclusively use in-house labor starting January 1.

Earlier this year, after AP reported on a slave island in Indonesia where fishermen were caged when on shore, Greenpeace called for a boycott of Thai Union and its Chicken of the Sea brand in the U.S. On Monday, Greenpeace campaign director John Hocevar said Thai Union isn't doing enough.

"The company does just enough to weather the PR storm while continuing to profit off the backs of the migrant workers forced to work throughout its supply chains," he said.

The Thai Embassy in Washington released a statement in response to the AP stories, saying the government will take action against those found to be involved in illegal activities.

"We are determined to ensure that the country's seafood supply chain is free of human trafficking and forced labor," it said.

The statement said the government has enacted laws to crack down on unlawful labor practices in seafood-processing factories, and will work with international and local partners to raise awareness and boost inspections.

Most U.S. customers said they're sticking with their Thai distributors, and Gavin Gibbons, a spokesman for National Fisheries Institute, which represents about 75 percent of the U.S. seafood industry, said boycotting Thailand is not the answer.

"If you don't buy seafood from there you're not in the conversation anymore about labor, you don't have the ability to fix it. You don't have an ability to push for change. You don't have an ability to say, 'These are my policies and if you don't abide by these policies and if you don't let third party auditors in, then you're going to lose access to this market,'" he said.

Buddy Galetti, president of Southwind Foods, a smaller importer in Los Angeles, disagreed.

"I guarantee you that if Wal-Mart and Kroger and Red Lobster stopped buying from Thailand until this got fixed, I think pretty soon Thailand would have no choice but to really deal with it," he said, adding he rarely buys Thai goods. "The large corporations are the ones who act like the pope as far as sustainability and human rights, but then they go out and buy from the main culprits."

AP's findings surprised some consumers. "I've bought bags of shrimp before at the market but never really looked at the label. I guess I should start looking, huh?" said Chris York, of Kensington, New Hampshire, a self-described seafood lover.

That was the advice of the U.S. State Department's new anti-trafficking ambassador Susan Coppedge. She said consumers should inform themselves, and can check the government-backed website slaveryfootprint.org and Labor Department publications before they spend "to make sure they're not made with forced slave labor."

EU DEMANDS SEAFOOD SLAVERY REFORM
Brussels, Friday, December 18, 2015

The European Union warned Thailand on Friday that it should "promptly" address the human rights and slavery issues that have dogged its seafood industry if it wants to stave off an EU seafood import ban.

Several investigative reports by The Associated Press focused on slavery in the seafood industry and resulted in the rescue of 2,000 men this year, highlighting longstanding abuses in Thai fisheries.

Thailand is a major exporter of seafood, with yearly revenues of almost 5 billion euros ($5.4 billion), and an EU ban would seriously affect the industry.

EU Fisheries Commissioner Karmenu Vella said even though the 28-nation bloc was primarily assessing Thailand's improvements in stamping out illegal fishing, there was no sidestepping the slavery issue.

Thailand, the world's third-largest seafood exporter, was given a warning by the EU in April to improve its fisheries practices or face an export ban to the wealthy European bloc. Annual Thai fish exports to the EU are estimated to be worth between 575 million and 730 million euros ($624 million to $792 million).

"We are still assessing whether Thailand has made sufficient progress in delivering on the actions" it was asked to take in April, Vella told reporters Friday.

"Regarding human rights, slavery on board and so on - yes, apart from the fishing issues, the Commission also believes that Thailand should also address promptly the human rights issues," he replied to a question from the AP.

The EU wants nations to be able to track their vessels and make sure they declare their catches to promote sustainable fishing and counter overfishing. The Commission is not expected to make a ruling on the Thai issue until late next month.

Vella spoke during a visit from Ghanean Fisheries Minister Sherry Ayittey, who noted that her nation was once penalized with such a ban.

European Union Commissioner for Fisheries Karmenu Vella, right, and Ghana's Minister of Fisheries Sherry Ayittey participate in a media conference at EU headquarters in Brussels, December 18, 2015. (AP Photo/Francois Walschaerts)

"It was like a wake-up call," Ayittey said. "It was necessary. It helped us to reshape our own governance of the fisheries sector."

Beyond illegal fishing though, Thailand also faces the slavery issue.

In the U.S., Congressman Emanuel Cleaver, a Democrat from Missouri, wrote to the Labor Department and the Food and Drug Administration this week demanding investigations after the AP investigated the shrimp peeling industry as well.

"I am deeply concerned for the welfare of adult and children shrimp peelers in Thailand, who are forced to work in one of the most abhorrent slavery schemes of the 21st century," he wrote.

Grocery and seafood organizations, meanwhile, say suppliers have to take responsibility for eliminating labor abuses in the fishing industry.

"In the case of the Thai shrimp industry, this means that simple audits and inspections of third-party shrimp peeling houses will not suffice, as corrupt police and inspectors turn a blind eye to abuses," said John Sackton in a report for Progressive Grocer.

TOP AWARD FOR AP FISH SLAVES REPORTING
AP Press Release, New York, September 28, 2015

Four Associated Press journalists will receive the gold award in the ninth annual Barlett & Steele Awards for Investigative Business Journalism for their work exposing slavery in the fishing industry in Southeast Asia and connecting the practice to U.S. supermarkets and pet food companies.

The awards were announced Monday by the Donald W. Reynolds National Center for Business Journalism at Arizona State University.

AP Executive Editor Kathleen Carroll said, "We are extremely proud of this work because it is leading to real change in the Southeast Asian fishing industry and the products that wind up in American households. What change? As of today, more than 2,000 slaves have been freed from the bondage as a direct result of the AP's reporting.

"Think about that. In 2015, journalism has freed 2,000 slaves. That is remarkable.

"Maggie, Robin, Esther and Martha are brilliant, resourceful, persistent and courageous journalists. They were supported by many other creative and committed colleagues and led by an excellent editor, Mary Rajkumar. Their work has the investigative rigor and impact that Don Barlett and Jim Steele have long represented."

The four — Robin McDowell, Margie Mason, Martha Mendoza and Esther Htusan — won the top award for a series of stories documenting how hundreds of men were working as slave labor, many of whom had not seen their homes and families in years.

Their investigative reporting linked slave-caught seafood to major supermarkets and pet food companies in the U.S.

"This was a gripping story with great reporting, and especially noteworthy was how careful the reporters were with its outcome by protecting the names of the slaves as they interviewed them and then notified authorities," said the judges, as quoted in the Reynolds Center announcement.

The $5,000 gold award will be presented on November 16 at the Walter Cronkite School of Journalism and Mass Communication at ASU in Phoenix.

CITATIONS AND BYLINES

Chapter 1. WHO CAUGHT THE FISH YOU BOUGHT?

NO ESCAPE
Ambon, Indonesia, Saturday, June 14, 2014
By Margie Mason

OVERFISHING DRIVING SLAVERY
Samut Sakhon, Wednesday, February 25, 2015
By Robin McDowell and Margie Mason

Chapter 2. BENJINA ISLAND

LIVING IN A CAGE
Benjina, Indonesia, Wednesday, March 25, 2015
By Robin McDowell, Margie Mason, and Martha Mendoza

Chapter 3. SILVER SEA STORY

TRACKING WITH TECHNOLOGY
Yangon, Myanmar, Monday, July 27, 2015
By Robin McDowell, Martha Mendoza, and Margie Mason

SEIZING THE SILVER SEA 2
Jakarta, Indonesia, Friday, August 14, 2015
By Margie Mason

ARRESTING SLAVERS
Sabang, Indonesia, Saturday, September 26, 2015
By Fakhrurradzie Gade, Margie Mason, and Robin McDowell

Chapter 4. IN SPITE OF THE LAW

INDUCED ACTION
Benjina, Indonesia, Friday, April 3, 2015
By Robin McDowell and Margie Mason

14 YEARS AND THEY ARE STILL DOING IT
Washington, Wednesday, April 22, 2015
By Martha Mendoza

INDONESIAN POLICE ARREST SEVEN
Jakarta, Indonesia, Wednesday, May 13, 2015
By Margie Mason

TRAFFICKING BROKERS ARRESTED
Bangkok, Thailand, Wednesday, July 1, 2015
By Thanyarat Doksone

SEAFOOD SUPPLIER LABOR ABUSE ADMITTED
Washington, Monday, November 23, 2015
By Martha Mendoza

THE AP EMERGENCY RELIEF FUND

When Hurricane Katrina hit the Gulf Coast in 2005, many Associated Press staffers and their families were personally affected. AP employees rallied to help these colleagues by setting up the AP Emergency Relief Fund, which has become a source of crucial assistance for the past 10 years.

Established as an independent 501(c)(3), the Fund helps AP staffers who have suffered damage or losses as a result of conflict or natural disasters. These grants are used to rebuild homes, move to safe houses and repair and replace bomb-damaged belongings.

The AP matches all gifts in full and also donates the net proceeds from AP Essentials, AP's company store, to the Fund.

HOW TO GIVE

In order to be ready to help the moment emergencies strike, the Fund relies on the generous and ongoing support of the extended AP community. All donations are matched in full by The Associated Press and can be made any time at http://www.ap.org/relieffund and are tax deductible.

On behalf of the AP staffers and families who receive aid in times of crisis, the AP Emergency Relief Fund Directors and Officers thank you.

ALSO AVAILABLE FROM AP EDITIONS

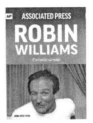

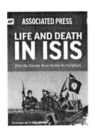

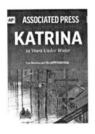

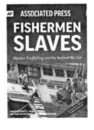

CPSIA information can be obtained at www.ICGtesting.com
Printed in the USA
BVOW05s1543050216

435692BV00003B/4/P